OVERVIEW

Overview

How do you know if one of your employees is underperforming? And at what point does this become a real problem? Managers, supervisors, and business leaders must be able to intervene before employee performance issues hamper the success of their organizations.

Performance problems in the workplace can be isolated incidents or symptoms of deeper patterns. It can be easy to miss these problems or to underestimate their impact. However, various indicators – such as employees missing deadlines or regularly being late for work – can alert you to possible performance issues and help you decide whether they constitute genuine performance problems.

As a manager, you should have warning systems in place so you can detect potential performance problems early. If you avoid problems before they grow, you can prevent them from having serious consequences – for your organization and often for the employees involved.

In this book, you'll learn how to detect a performance problem as early as possible. You'll find out how to identify genuine performance problems and the sources of information that can help you do this. You'll then find out how to determine a performance problem's nature and its seriousness. Finally, you'll learn how to accurately diagnose the causes of the problem, which is essential if you're to formulate an appropriate response.

Telling employees that their work doesn't meet the required standards or that they're underperforming isn't an easy task. A direct report who's not performing well could be a friend or someone who's highly emotional, making the job even harder. Many managers and supervisors are tempted to avoid it, until it's too late to fix the problem.

In this book, you'll learn about the benefits of handling minor to moderate performance problems early on, as they arise. You'll also learn how to identify an appropriate level of intervention, based on how pervasive or serious a performance problem is.

Once you've identified the type of intervention that's called for to address a performance problem, you need to handle the issue appropriately. In this book, you'll learn about the sequence of steps you should follow to communicate performance issues to employees, with practical examples of how to do this sensitively and effectively. You'll also be given the opportunity to practice this type of communication yourself in a simulated situation.

Finally, you'll learn about both fast fixes and long-term solutions to different types of performance problems.

Ultimately, this book should help you improve employees' performance and morale, benefiting both them and your organization.

Suppose you're the manager of an employee who's been arriving at work over 20 minutes late nearly every day. You've explained that this is a problem, but the employee continues arriving late. It's time to take action. If an employee continues failing to meet expectations, it's important to take decisive steps, rather than waiting for the problem to escalate further.

If you don't take action in response to repeated performance problems, the problems are likely to become more entrenched.

Failing to act may also undermine your authority, or make it appear to other employees that undesirable behavior is actually acceptable.

Finally, if you don't act, it may be much harder to take necessary and more drastic action later. For example, the employee who always arrives 20 minutes late in the mornings begins to take longer lunches and sometimes fails to return to the office. He offers no explanation. If you have no records of the previous problems or of formal steps you took to address them, it may be hard to justify dismissing the employee.

When a performance problem persists, what's required is progressive discipline. This approach involves imposing increasingly severe penalties on employees each time they fail to improve their performance, despite a manager's efforts to assist them.

In this book, you'll learn about progressive discipline and when it's appropriate. You'll also learn how to implement its three stages:

- when and how to issue employees with verbal warnings, including examples of the language you should use,
- when and how to issue written warnings, and how to ensure that these warnings are effective, and
- when and how to issue a final written warning.

After completing this book, you should be able to implement progressive discipline when it's appropriate and in a way that benefits your employees and your organization.

When employees fail to meet work-related expectations, it can have negative consequences for them, for colleagues who depend on their work, and for their organization as a whole. This is why it's critical for managers to be proactive about performance management. They need to prevent problems when possible and address problems quickly when they do occur.

Performance management is an ongoing dialog between employer and employee about how the employee can achieve the best results. It involves planning and monitoring performance, and communicating feedback.

The process of managing performance should be collaborative, not prescriptive. It should encourage employees to explore their strengths and weaknesses on a regular basis and to identify how their organization can support them in reaching higher levels of performance.

It should also ensure employees can relate their jobs to the organizational goals of the company. An understanding of the "bigger picture" helps employees do the job more efficiently, according to expectations.

Even the best performance management can't guarantee that problems won't ever occur. But an effective system can prevent many types of problems. It can also ensure you detect performance issues early, so you can address them before they grow into more serious problems.

In this book, you'll learn how to use performance management to prevent performance problems. You'll explore several key concepts and techniques:

- what performance management involves and how it can help prevent performance problems,
- how to plan performance in ways that motivate employees,
- how best to monitor employees' actual performance in relation to the desired, or planned, performance, and
- how best to deliver feedback to employees about their performance.

CHAPTER 1 - RECOGNIZING AND DIAGNOSING PROBLEM PERFORMANCE

CHAPTER 1 - Recognizing and Diagnosing Problem Performance

SECTION 1 - DETECTING PERFORMANCE PROBLEMS

SECTION 1 - Detecting Performance Problems

It's important to detect and address performance problems before they affect an entire organization. You can gather information about employees' performance by collecting specific data, communicating openly, and observing the employees directly.

A true performance problem involves a discrepancy between actual and desired performance. You can use a variety of sources of information to determine what constitutes desired performance in your organization.

DETECTING PERFORMANCE PROBLEMS

Detecting performance problems

Andrew is a copy editor for a publishing house. He's often late for work, regularly misses deadlines, and makes careless errors. The situation is worsening and his manager is concerned.

Question

What do you think are possible consequences of Andrew's poor performance?

Options:

1. Delays for layout artists
2. Low-quality work, resulting in complaints from customers
3. Poor team cohesion among editors and writers
4. Better performance by others, who make up for Andrew's faults
5. A more relaxed workplace culture

Answer

Option 1: This is a correct option. Roles in a production flow are often interdependent, so problems in one area affect other areas too. For example, layout artists may have to wait for the copy that Andrew submits late.

Option 2: This is a correct option. Poor work practices result in work of lower quality, and this can harm a company's reputation.

Option 3: This option is correct. Andrew's poor performance may make him disliked and so less productive as a team member. This would lead to poor cohesion among the editors and writers.

Option 4: This is an incorrect option. Andrew's poor performance is most likely to have a negative impact on others, possibly leading to conflict and making it more difficult for them to do their jobs well.

Option 5: This option is incorrect. Andrew's attitude is more likely to cause conflict – with other employees having to do the work Andrew can't finish – than to result in a more relaxed work environment.

Poor employee performance can happen in any organization. It can occur as an isolated incident or be part of an ongoing pattern. Managers need to detect poor performance early. They then need to understand what's causing the problem and try to find a solution for it.

Poor performance happens for different reasons. Employees may feel bored or unmotivated, or they may lack the necessary skills.

Alternatively, the problem may lie with the employees' managers.

A performance problem can be described as a failure to meet particular standards. For example, an employee's behavior may fail to meet the standards for employee interactions, or for employee-manager interactions. It may also violate policy-related standards or work standards.

Standards for employee interactions

An example of failing to meet the standards for employee interactions is annoying coworkers through behavior such as constant rude remarks or loud laughter in an open-plan office.

Standards for employee-manager interactions

A subordinate who challenges the authority of a manager may be violating standards that govern the interactions between employees and managers. This can undermine a manager's function and disrupt work flow.

Policy-related standards

Examples of failing to meet policy-related standards include absenteeism, misuse of company resources, and safety violations.

Work standards

Examples of failing to meet work standards include missing deadlines and producing shoddy work.

Managers should have early warning systems in place so they can detect and address performance problems before they affect the organization. When there is a marked disparity between an employee's behavior and how you expect that employee to behave, you should intervene.

However, early intervention requires sensitivity. Occasionally managers rush to a judgment about why an employee is underperforming and then act without asking enough questions. This can result in an employee being unfairly disciplined or even dismissed, sometimes while the original problem persists.

Managers should look out for negative performance indicators in employees' self-management. They should also observe their ability to manage others, how they manage their work performance, and their workplace relationships, communication, and customer relations.

Self-management

Indicators of poor self-management include needing to be supervised all the time, not taking initiative, not keeping skills up to date, fixating on symptoms instead of addressing the causes of a problem, and making short-sighted decisions.

Ability to manage others

Signs of poor performance in managing others include disrupting a team, not accepting feedback, blaming others unreasonably, insisting on one's own way, ignoring team goals, and failing to win respect.

Work performance

Indicators of poor work performance include not meeting deadlines, failing to heed instructions, regularly doing the bare minimum, being absent-minded, making shoddy or unacceptable mistakes, and relying too much on others.

Workplace relationships

Signs that an employee has poor relationships in the workplace include the employee being indifferent to others, not working with other team members but trying to get things done alone, presenting weak proposals, and showing courtesy only when there's something to gain from it.

Communication

Indicators of weak communication include not conveying requirements, writing verbose or unclear reports, making presentations that are difficult to follow, struggling to get to the point, and frequently reaching wrong conclusions.

Customer relations

Indicators of unsatisfactory customer relations include failing to show empathy for customers, ignoring customer requests, passing on requests to others that could have been addressed, being slow to respond to customer grievances, and regularly receiving negative customer feedback.

If you notice any of these signs in an employee, you should consider whether there's really a problem, how serious or urgent the problem is, and what the root causes are.

As a manager, it's your responsibility to gather information about your employees' performance as part of an ongoing monitoring process. Just conducting annual or biannual performance appraisals isn't enough if you're to detect and address problems early on.

You can gather information about employees' performance by collecting specific data, communicating with employees, and observing employees directly.

Collecting data

You can collect specific data throughout the year to gain a general idea of staff performance. For example, you can monitor the performance of sales staff by tracking their weekly and monthly sales figures.

Communicating with employees

It's essential to communicate regularly with employees to stay aware of their progress. Communicating openly can also help ensure that employees feel comfortable in alerting you to problems they're having.

Observing employees

You can observe employees directly to gather information about their performance. For example, a tour of company premises may show you how busy employees are and give you insights into employee morale.

Question

Which are examples of appropriate ways to detect problems with an employee's performance?

Options:

1. Walk around the office when your staff members are at work

2. Conduct annual performance reviews

3. Listen to what others have to say about the employee in informal conversations

4. Compile a record of the employee's monthly output

5. Chat with the employee to find out how this person is doing

Answer

Option 1: This is a correct option. Observing employees directly is a good way of gathering information about their performance.

Option 2: This is an incorrect option. Performance reviews can alert you to problems, but they may not reveal problem performance. Instead, you should monitor performance on an ongoing basis.

Option 3: This option is incorrect. Managers need to base their decisions about employees' performance on more than just rumors and gossip.

Option 4: This is a correct option. Collecting data such as monthly output figures is a good way to gather information about the performance of individual employees.

Option 5: This option is correct. Communicating regularly with employees keeps you aware of their progress and creates an atmosphere of trust.

IDENTIFYING PERFORMANCE PROBLEMS

Identifying performance problems

A true performance problem involves a discrepancy between actual and desired performance. To analyze a possible performance problem objectively, you should start by asking yourself whose performance is in doubt. Then ask what the employee's actual performance is and what the desired performance is.

Whose performance is in doubt?

It's important to verify whose performance is in doubt to prevent misinterpretation. For example, an employee may be producing less work than assigned – but this might be because the supervisor is assigning the employee too many tasks.

What is the actual performance?

It's important to determine what the employee's actual performance is. For example, you might track exactly what a copywriter does during a work day. You might discover that the copywriter works only for about 4 hours a day and spends the remaining time socializing.

What is the desired performance?

It's not enough to know how an employee is actually performing. You also have to know how the employee should be performing. Then you can determine whether there's a significant gap between actual and desired performance.

Suppose a copywriter produces 10 pages of copy a week. It's clear that this is a problem only if copywriters are expected to submit a minimum of 12 or more pages per week, and other copywriters consistently do so.

As a manager, you shouldn't confuse a performance problem with its repercussions. The negative consequences of a problem may cause difficulties but they aren't the problem itself.

For example, an employee in an engineering company refuses to work in a team. She doesn't share tasks and disrespects her colleagues. This has caused tension in the laboratory.

The disunity is a negative consequence but the problem is really the divide between this employee's actual attitude and the one that's desired.

It's also important to realize that some performance discrepancies you detect may not be the fault of the employee. They may result from poor understanding, unclear guidelines, or insufficient resources. Regardless of the causes – which you'll determine at a later stage – you should still identify such discrepancies as performance problems.

To recognize a true performance discrepancy, you have to know what should be happening in your organization. Various sources of information can help you determine this:

- job performance standards, which define minimum requirements for employees and may be determined scientifically or through experience - An example of job performance standards are minimum sales per day.
- work expectations, which define average or expected output rather than minimum requirements - An example of work expectations are average sales.
- key performance indicators, or KPIs, which are measures of types of performance considered key to a particular organization's success – for instance meeting deadlines
- key result areas for your organization – or areas in which strong performance is considered critical, such as sales or security, and
- performance criteria, or the criteria your organization uses to assess employee performance – including specific skills and behaviors - Whether an employee has met the performance criteria, may be discussed during performance appraisals.

Other sources of organizational information can help you detect performance discrepancies:

- your organization's code of conduct, which defines acceptable and unacceptable types of employee behavior,
- your organization's policies and guidelines, as established by senior management,
- relevant benchmarks, which are industry bests or desired levels of achievement against which performance can be measured, and

- your organization's goals, objectives, and overall vision, so that you can determine whether individual employees' performance is in line with these.

Question

Which are descriptions of performance problems?

Options:

1. Work production levels below minimum
2. A habit of insulting colleagues
3. Routinely missed deadlines
4. Failure to understand company policies
5. Disharmony in a work group

Answer

Option 1: This option is correct. Employees must meet job performance standards that define minimum requirements – the volume of work they're expected to produce, for example.

Option 2: This is a correct option. An employee who constantly insults others violates the standards that govern normal employee interactions, and may be violating a company's code of conduct. This is a performance problem that may disrupt several people's work.

Option 3: This is a correct option. Meeting deadlines is usually a key performance indicator for an organization – and regular failure to meet deadlines is a performance problem.

Option 4: This is an incorrect option. An employee may fail to understand company policies, but until this results in performance that falls below expectations, lack of understanding isn't itself a performance problem.

Option 5: This option is incorrect. Group disharmony is a consequence of a performance problem, rather than the problem itself.

If you're clear about the expectations and standards that employees must meet, any departure from these standards will set off alarm bells. However, you must make sure the performance discrepancy can be observed and measured, and that you don't base your judgment just on "a bad feeling" you have about an employee.

Case Study: Question 1 of 1

Scenario

For your convenience, the case study is repeated with each question.

You're currently analyzing four employees, each with various performance issues.

Paula

Paula is a designer. She is talented but her manager has recorded her repeated failure to meet departmental deadlines. When confronted about this, she becomes aggressive.

Audrey

Audrey is a desk clerk and a single mother. Recently she's started occasionally bringing her one-year old daughter to work. Audrey's manager has said this is only a problem if it disturbs others and so far no-one has complained.

Rick

Rick is an account executive in an advertising agency. Apparently, he has antagonized the creative team so much that nobody wants to work with him. The creative director has noticed that people have been avoiding him for over three months.

Gina

Gina is a travel agent. The agency recently replaced its booking software with a new and more complex system. All employees received training on how to use the new system. However, Gina is struggling to get used to the new software, and her boss is hearing customers complain of double bookings and failed cancellations.

Question

Which employees are exhibiting genuine and properly detected performance problems?

Options:

1. Paula
2. Audrey
3. Rick
4. Gina

Answer

Option 1: This is a correct option. Paula's manager has objectively recorded her failure to meet deadlines. Together with her aggressive response, this indicates a performance problem.

Option 2: This option is incorrect. Audrey's manager agreed that she could bring her child to work − so she hasn't violated any standards or failed to meet expectations by doing this.

Option 3: This is an incorrect option. The team's response to Rick is just a consequence of a problem. The real problem is whatever Rick is doing that causes this response.

Option 4: This is a correct option. There's a discrepancy between desired behavior and Gina's actual behavior. Customer complaints are an objective indicator of a performance problem. In this example, the cause of the problem is Gina's difficulty in learning how to use new software.

x

SECTION 2 - DETERMINING THE NATURE OF PROBLEMS

SECTION 2 - Determining the Nature of Problems

After detecting a workplace performance problem, you need to ask questions to further assess the scope, frequency, and impact of the problem.

To be effective, your questioning should follow several guidelines – such as meeting involved employees in private and remaining neutral when questioning. By finding out about a problem's scope, frequency, and impact, you can better determine how best to solve the problem.

ESSENTIAL ELEMENTS OF A PROBLEM

Essential elements of a problem

The first step in managing employee performance problems is detecting them when they occur. But once you've detected a problem, you can't rely on assumptions about what that problem is. Before you can address a problem effectively, you need to find out more about it.

You'll need to explore three essential elements of the problem – its scope, frequency, and impact.

Scope

The scope of a problem is its extent – including what the problem involves, where it's occurring, and who's involved in or affected by it.

Frequency

The frequency of a problem is how often the problem occurs.

Impact

The impact of a problem is its effects or the consequences it has.

These important elements help you to determine how urgent a problem is, which helps you decide what actions to take next. For relatively minor problems, you might choose just to monitor the situation or to have a casual conversation with the employee exhibiting the problem behavior.

But for critical problems, or those that could rapidly deteriorate, you need to intervene immediately and you may need to take disciplinary action. If a performance problem falls outside your area of responsibility, you need to bring it to the attention of the relevant people.

For example, if an employee is having psychological issues, you should bring in the company's counselor, if one is available, or human resources manager. Of if you know an employee is exposing your company's trade secrets, you should alert security and the company's legal team.

QUESTIONING TECHNIQUES

Questioning techniques

One of the best ways to study the scope, frequency, and impact of a workplace problem is to speak to and ask questions of those who are involved – both the employee exhibiting the problem behavior and those affected by the problem. This isn't always easy though because raising questions about a problem can provoke emotional responses.

To make your questioning process sensitive yet effective, you should follow several guidelines:

- meet privately,
- remain neutral,
- use only simple, focused questions, and
- give the employees time to answer.

Meet privately

If you need to discuss a performance problem with an employee, you should always meet with the employee privately, where other colleagues won't overhear your conversation. If necessary, include other relevant parties – such as a human resources representative.

Ensuring privacy helps protect the dignity and reputation of the employee. It can also give this person the confidence to speak honestly, making it more likely you'll get accurate answers.

Remain neutral

To get accurate and honest answers, show the employee that you're neutral and fair. Don't let your own inherent biases or perceptions influence the questions you ask or your responses. Seek out the real answers, instead of the answers you want to hear.

You can demonstrate neutrality by adopting a no-nonsense, business-like demeanor, with a careful balance between formality and friendliness. To be fair during the process, avoid assigning blame and don't take sides when different parties are discussed.

Use simple, focused questions

To avoid digressions and misunderstandings, ask clearly defined questions that are to the point and require straightforward answers. Limit each question to a specific objective and make sure that each question addresses a relevant topic.

Give time to answer

If you pressure employees for answers, chances are they'll give you quick, inaccurate responses rather than the accurate information you're seeking. To avoid this, give employees time to fully comprehend what you've asked and to think of their responses.

Roy, a software company manager, notices that one team always runs far over schedule and often delivers projects that clients aren't happy with. After some investigation, he realizes that most of the delays and client complaints can be attributed to Patrick, the team's systems analyst.

Patrick often relies on his own intuition and opinions rather than paying careful attention to stated client requirements. When this causes problems, he asks programmers to rework the product instead of admitting his errors.

The company's other systems analysts – who work in different teams – are more responsive to client input, and so don't tend to have these rework problems.

But Patrick refuses to acknowledge that his own work style is the problem. Instead. he claims that his team's projects are more complex than those assigned to the other teams and cites this as the cause of delays and extra work.

Question

Roy meets with Patrick's team members, then decides to take further action.

How should Roy address the issue?

Options:

1. Arrange an open session with Patrick and all other employees in the conference room

2. Arrange a private meeting with Patrick in his office

3. Arrange a meeting with Patrick and the company's finance manager in his office

Answer

Option 1: This option is incorrect. Roy should meet with Patrick in private, rather than embarrassing him in front of other employees and potentially preventing him from speaking honestly.

Option 2: This is the correct option. A private meeting is best. This will protect Patrick from embarrassment and help ensure he has the confidence to speak honestly.

Option 3: This is an incorrect option. It would be inappropriate to include people who aren't relevant to the problem. Instead Roy should meet with Patrick privately.

Several actions could undermine the effectiveness of your questioning. These include apologizing, leading the employee, revealing personal history, losing your neutrality, and wrapping up inappropriately.

Apologizing

Questioning is part of your job, so you shouldn't apologize for having to do it. Apologizing may cause the employee to take your questioning lightly or to give you inaccurate answers.

Leading

Avoid asking employees leading questions or indicating your unspoken thoughts or preferences through your physical reactions. You may influence employees to change their answers to suit what they think you want to hear.

You should ask open-ended questions and keep your facial expressions, body language, and tone of voice neutral. Don't reveal an obvious preference or dislike for certain responses. For example, don't aggressively ask, "Didn't we give you more than enough time to finish the assignment?" Rather, calmly ask, "What prevented you from finishing the assignment on time?"

Revealing personal history

You should never try to win an employee's trust by revealing embarrassing aspects of your own personal history.

If an employee is doing something wrong and you made a similar mistake in the past, it can be tempting to reveal your past in an attempt to bring out the employee's honesty. But admitting such past guilt isn't appropriate in a business setting. If you've committed a similar offence in the past, employees might think you have no moral right to admonish them about it.

Losing neutrality

To remain neutral, don't let the employee draw you into an argument. To sidestep your questions, employees may argue or reveal their own grievances. Resist such tactics and try not to be swayed by emotions.

Also guard against letting assumptions, presumptions, and foregone conclusions affect your judgment.

Wrapping up inappropriately

When closing a questioning session, don't rush to make judgments about what was discussed and don't make promises about actions you'll take to resolve the problem.

Instead, tell the employee that you'll take some time to consider the conversation and other information, and that you'll speak to the employee again once you've come to a conclusion and decision.

Case Study: Question 1 of 2

Scenario

Roy, the software company manager, arranges a private meeting with Patrick in his office. Roy hopes to address Patrick's problematic behaviors – missing deadlines, failing to listen to client requirements, and covering up problems.

Answer the questions in any order.

Question

Which are appropriate examples of what Roy can say to Patrick?

Options:

1. "I'm sorry I have to interview you like this, but it's company policy."

2. "Why do you say that your team's projects are more complex than other teams' projects?"

3. "How closely do you listen to client requirements? Take a few moments to think about it."

4. "I understand what you're saying, but you still haven't convinced me."

Answer

Option 1: This is an incorrect option. It's inappropriate for Roy to apologize for questioning Patrick about performance. Doing this is his job – and being apologetic may prevent Patrick from taking what Roy says seriously.

Option 2: This option is correct. This question is neutral in its phrasing. It doesn't criticize Patrick's claim, making it more likely that Patrick will respond openly and honestly.

Option 3: This is a correct option. This approach gives Patrick time to consider his answer, rather than pressuring him for an instant response.

Option 4: This option is incorrect. This statement is inappropriate because it indicates that Roy isn't neutral – he begins the meeting with a presumption and is still letting that presumption affect his thinking. This is likely to make Patrick defensive.

Case Study: Question 2 of 2

Which are appropriate statements or questions about Patrick's problematic behavior?

Options:

1. "Think of a project problem you encountered recently. How did you handle that problem?"

2. "How come you don't take detailed notes when clients are giving you their requirements?"

3. "I've also missed a fair share of deadlines in the past, but..."

4. "How would you rate your team's ability to meet its deadlines?"

5. "To be honest, these excuses you're giving aren't very credible."

Answer

Option 1: This option is correct. This question is simple and focuses on a single point – how Patrick handled a problem.

Option 2: This is an incorrect option. This question is inappropriate because it's leading. It implies a pre-judgment of Patrick's note-taking practices.

Option 3: This option is incorrect. This statement is inappropriate because it reveals Roy's personal history. He shouldn't admit to missing deadlines himself in the context of attempting to address Patrick's performance problems.

Option 4: This is a correct option. This question is suitably neutral and to the point. It's likely to encourage Patrick to respond openly.

Option 5: This is an incorrect option. This is an inappropriate statement because it's not neutral – Roy is passing judgment rather than focusing on obtaining accurate information about the problem.

ASSESSING SCOPE, FREQUENCY, AND IMPACT

Assessing scope, frequency, and impact

When asking questions about a performance problem, it's important to be clear about exactly what information you're searching for. You should design your questions to determine the problem's scope, frequency, and impact.

To determine the scope of a performance problem, you need to be specific and precise in identifying the problem areas.

There are five main types of questions that should form the basis for your queries:

1. What happened?
2. When did it happen?
3. Where did it happen?
4. Who was involved?
5. Why did it happen?

Defining the "what" helps you to identify the specific discrepancy between what should have happened and what actually did. This is a particularly important starting point because it separates perceptions from facts.

Perceptions

Perceptions are people's personal understandings of events. They're shaped by people's world views and backgrounds. They're subjective and can be debated.

Facts

Facts are objective records of actual events – described without bias or opinion. Facts can be independently verified and aren't influenced by people's individual views.

A sound diagnostic process is based on facts. It's inappropriate to rely on perceptions or assumptions because doing this can cause you to diagnose a problem incorrectly. For example, a manager may accuse an employee of never starting work on time. In the manager's mind, the problem is the employee's disregard for time.

However, the employee may have a legitimate reason for being late, such as having to take unreliable public transportation. An effective diagnostic process should strip away any faulty perceptions by defining the actual problem – in this case, simply the fact that the employee is often late for work.

It's important to identify exactly which employees are involved in the problem. You should be specific in this step, because your diagnostic process can fail if you're too vague or you don't identify the relevant employees correctly.

Also consider the context for the problem. Does it occur only under specific circumstances, or is it an ongoing, general problem? You can ask whether the problem occurs throughout the work day, or only at the end of the day. This information can help you pinpoint the root cause of the problem.

Question

Employees in your company's Sales Department have been performing poorly recently and you're trying to define the problem.

Which statement is most effective in defining the problem?

Options:

1. The Sales Department's sales figures dropped last month

2. Last month, Jim, Allan, and Rosie sold half as many units as their other sales colleagues

3. Jim, Allan, and Rosie don't put in as much effort as their colleagues

Answer

Option 1: This option is incorrect. This statement uses a fact to describe the problem, but it's vague about the employees involved.

Option 2: This is the correct option. This statement identifies three specific employees causing the problem, and uses a specific fact to describe that problem.

Option 3: This is an incorrect option. Although this statement identifies specific employees, it uses a perception – rather than facts – to describe the problem.

To assess the frequency of the problem, first check whether the problem is the result of an accident or misunderstanding. For example, the editor of a newsletter finds that one of the writers used the Courier New font, instead of the required Courier PS font.

By investigating the issue, the editor discovers that the writer made the mistake because she misread the editorial style guide. But she has since corrected the mistake, and no further action is needed.

After ruling out accidents and misunderstandings, you should ask how often the problem has occurred. Was there a single occurrence or repeated occurrence of the relevant behavior? Does it form a continuing pattern?

Single occurrence

If a problem behavior has occurred just once – provided that it isn't an extremely serious violation – it shouldn't be dealt with too harshly because it's a first offence.

Repeated occurrence

A problem behavior may be repeated – either because the employee is unaware of the behavior or underestimates the seriousness of the problem – before a manager addresses it.

Continuing pattern

A problem behavior may become normal for an employee. This could occur especially if management fails to take strong enough action in response to early occurrences of the problem.

You should instigate disciplinary action if a problem behavior continues to occur even after the employee has been informed of the problem and your expectations, and informal interventions have been conducted.

You should also establish whether the problem behavior involves a serious policy violation – in which case even a single incident requires further attention. For example, an occurrence of behavior deemed to be sexual harassment should be addressed urgently.

Assessing the impact of a performance problem involves identifying its consequences. You should consider the problem's actual and potential consequences on people, organizational goals, and costs.

People

Ask what impact the problem has had on people. Has employee morale dropped? Have there been increased tensions or conflicts between employees? Is absenteeism on the rise?

Organizational goals

Ask whether the problem affects your company's ability to achieve its goals. What effect is the problem having on company performance and potential?

Costs

Ask what the problem is costing the company. Don't limit your analysis to financial costs only. Investigate other costs too, such as inefficiency, damage to the company's reputation, lost customers or business opportunities, and loss of talented employees.

Another good way to identify the impact of a performance problem is to consider the consequences of inaction. In other words, what could happen if you ignore the problem?

You might save resources by choosing not to take steps to resolve the problem. But in this case, what financial and other costs would you incur? Consider a wide range of areas, including finance, employee morale, training costs, time, and your organization's public reputation.

Also, if appropriate, gauge your colleagues' and employees' perception of how serious the problem is. The more people talk about it, the more serious the problem is likely to be.

Question

At your software company, you've noticed that developers and graphic designers have become increasingly agitated with each other over the past three weeks. In one incident, Carl, a designer, physically shoved Robert, a developer.

Match each aspect of the problem to the appropriate question for assessing it. Not all questions will have a match.

Options:

A. Scope

B. Frequency

C. Impact

Targets:

1. When the incident occurred, were Carl and Robert alone, or were there other employees involved in the conflict?

2. In the past three weeks, was this the first time that physical violence erupted between these employees?

3. How has this incident affected both teams' productivity?

4. What was the reason for Carl's aggression?

Answer

This question addresses scope because it aims to find out exactly who was involved in the incident.

This question addresses frequency because it aims to find out whether Carl's aggressive behavior is a one-time occurrence or has happened before.

This question addresses impact because it aims to find out what impact the incident has had – in this case, on the affected teams.

This question addresses the root cause of the incident. It doesn't address scope, frequency, or impact.

DRAWING CONCLUSIONS ABOUT A PROBLEM

Drawing conclusions about a problem

The conclusions you draw about a performance problem should depend on what you've learned about the problem's scope, frequency, and impact.

Scope

Scope helps you identify whether the problem is the employee or the situation. This knowledge then points you to what your solution should focus on.

For example, if all sales agents are struggling to cope with a new reporting system, the system might have flaws that need to be resolved. But if only one sales agent struggles, that agent may need mentoring.

Frequency

Frequency suggests the response you need to take, based on how often the problem occurs.

For single and repeated occurrences, you should have an informal discussion with the employee about the problem. For continuing patterns, intervene more formally.

Persistent issues may require disciplinary action in accordance with company policy – for example suspending or revoking certain privileges. For policy violations, intervene as per company policy, bearing in mind the seriousness of the violation and the context in which it occurred.

Impact

The impact of a performance problem indicates the scale and urgency of the response you need to take.

Even if a problem is relatively infrequent, you'll need to take serious action if its impact is substantial. For example, if an employee's behavior could result in the loss of an important client, it's urgent that you address the problem – even if it has occurred only once so far.

Suppose your small marketing company is under pressure to increase its output, so you're monitoring each employee's performance. The monthly output figures show that one of the graphic designers – Troy – has produced very much lower than average output for the past two months.

Because a new set of projects had particularly complex requirements, several designers suffered a small drop in productivity in the previous month. But Troy's fall in output is far more dramatic, and his work has a direct impact on the company's income stream.

Question

Consider the scope, frequency, and impact of Troy's performance problem.

What conclusions can you draw about this problem?

Options:

1. It's urgent that you further investigate the cause of last month's general design production dip

2. Failing to take action could have a negative impact on the company's financial stability

3. The problem is limited to Troy, rather than being a general one

4. You need to inform Troy that his recent output level is unacceptable and must improve

5. You can ignore the problem because Troy's underperformance isn't a disciplinary issue

Answer

Option 1: This option is incorrect. The underperformance problem is limited to Troy – it doesn't involve the designers in general. The general decrease was small and you already know the reason behind it.

Option 2: This is a correct option. Because the company is small, continued underperformance could have a major negative impact on the company's success.

Option 3: This option is correct. Although other designers' output dropped last month, none of them experienced drops as extreme or sustained as Troy's. So you need to give Troy individual attention to improve his performance.

Option 4: This is a correct option. Because this problem has occurred for two consecutive months and could become a continuing pattern, you need to make Troy aware of the problem and your expectations.

Option 5: This is an incorrect option. Because the problem is a repeated occurrence with high impact, you need to take action immediately.

SECTION 3 - DIAGNOSING ROOT CAUSES OF PROBLEMS

SECTION 3 - Diagnosing Root Causes of Problems

Accurately determining the causes of performance problems is the first step in finding the right solutions.

Guidelines for diagnosing the causes of a performance problem include involving the relevant employee, using good diagnostic techniques, looking for external causes before internal causes, and verifying that your conclusions are focused, complete, coherent, and impartial.

IMPORTANCE OF EFFECTIVE DIAGNOSIS

Importance of effective diagnosis

An administrative assistant in a large company is responsible for creating reports, scheduling appointments, updating a database, and answering calls. The assistant repeatedly fails to keep up with all these tasks and, in disciplinary sessions, his manager tells him he needs to improve his efficiency. Eventually the assistant is dismissed and a new person is hired – and it turns out that this person can't complete all the required tasks in the given time either.

The root cause of the problem was that the administrative assistant's job was badly designed. It included too much work for one person. Tasks not being completed were merely a symptom of this. Unfortunately, root causes aren't always easy to uncover, which is why the first administrative assistant was dismissed.

The manager's view that the administrative assistant was being inefficient was part of a bias. It was only once it was too late that the manager interpreted the situation, rather than the employee, as being the problem.

Three types of bias can distort your perceptions of a performance problem. These include attributional bias, self-serving bias, and what's known as the plausibility trap.

Attributional bias

Attributional bias involves overestimating an individual's characteristics as the cause of particular behavior and underestimating the context – or situation – as the cause.

For example, it's common to blame poor performance on an employee's personality when it's really a situation outside the employee's control, like poor job design, that's causing the problem.

Self-serving bias

Self-serving bias is a tendency to attribute our own successes to personal factors and failures to factors outside our control. It helps protect our self-esteem, but can prevent people from accepting responsibility for their mistakes.

Plausibility trap

The plausibility trap refers to people's tendency to accept the first credible scenario that comes to mind, even if it's false or incomplete, and then to use this as a point of reference for gathering new information.

Following specific guidelines can help prevent bias from blurring your judgment of employees' performance:

- involve the relevant employee in assessing performance,
- use objective diagnostic techniques to arrive at conclusions,

- look for external causes before internal causes of performance problems, and
- ensure your final diagnosis of any performance problem is focused, coherent, complete, and impartial.

Question

Why do you think it's important to follow the guidelines for diagnosing the causes of performance problems?

Options:

1. It helps prevent you from wasting time pursuing ineffective responses

2. It can help you overcome bias

3. It helps ensure that you don't miss problem causes that you can control

4. It can equip you to make changes that improve the performance of many employees

5. It fosters trust among employees

6. It can help ensure that fewer performance problems occur

7. It can make it unnecessary to instigate disciplinary action

Answer

Option 1: This option is correct. Following the guidelines can help ensure that you diagnose problems correctly and so don't waste time and effort on ineffective responses.

Option 2: This is the correct option. Following the guidelines can help you overcome the types of bias that often blur managers' judgment of the root causes of performance problems.

Option 3: This option is correct. Many performance problems can be traced to situational causes you can control. If you diagnose these problems accurately, you can take steps to overcome them.

Option 4: This is a correct option. Many root causes of performance problems are situational, or systemic. Accurately identifying these causes equips you to address them, potentially improving the performance of many employees.

Option 5: This option is correct. Employees are more likely to trust you if they know that you're objective and fair when evaluating their performance.

Option 6: This option is incorrect. The guidelines relate to diagnosing performance problems accurately, rather than preventing the problems from occurring initially.

Option 7: This is an incorrect option. The guidelines help ensure that you diagnose problems accurately. They don't affect the types of responses that are appropriate.

So following guidelines for diagnosing performance problems can have several benefits. It can prevent wasted time and effort, help you overcome bias, and help you trace problems to causes you can control. It can help you detect and resolve systemic problems. And it can help you foster trust in your objectivity.

GUIDELINES FOR DIAGNOSING PROBLEMS

Guidelines for diagnosing problems

Often the best source of knowledge about a performance problem is the employee who's experiencing the problem. That's why it's important to involve this person in diagnosing the problem and its root cause. Doing this can also make the employee more open to addressing the problem.

You need to diagnose a problem once you've detected it. So as part of the diagnosing process, you need to ask questions – and interview relevant witnesses – to investigate the what, where, when, who, and – most importantly – the why of the problem.

You should keep questions simple, open-ended, and focused, ensuring they call for straightforward responses and aren't confusing.

You should also ensure that you give the employee time to think and to formulate well-considered responses, instead of rushing this person into giving quick answers.

It may be appropriate to interview other employees who have relevant information about a performance problem – for example, because they witnessed it or were affected by it. It's important to do this discreetly.

Once you've gathered initial information about a performance problem, you can use various diagnostic techniques to learn more and to help determine the problem's root cause. Two examples of these techniques are brainstorming and a technique known as the "five whys."

Brainstorming

Brainstorming involves two or more people thinking of as many ideas as possible in a short time. Usually a question is asked, and those in the group try to provide possible answers. Ideas are recorded but not evaluated and people are encouraged to build on one another's ideas. Once the session has finished, the group may determine which ideas are the best.

Brainstorming with colleagues, involved employees, or other appropriate parties can be a useful way of generating ideas about the causes of a performance problem.

Five whys

The technique known as the "five whys" involves using a series of "why" questions to drill down to the real cause of a problem. In practice, you might ask fewer than five of these questions – or more than five – before arriving at a conclusion. You can use the technique yourself, with an employee, or in a group.

For example, you might start with a question like "Why does John come to work late?" and an obvious answer like "He says he often over-sleeps." You might continue as follows – "Why is John waking up late in the mornings? He's tired. Why is John always tired? He often works late. Why is John having to work late? He has lots of extra work. Why is John having to do so much extra work?" This may point you directly to the root cause of a performance problem.

Question

Which are examples of good approaches for diagnosing the cause of an employee's performance problem?

Options:

1. Ask the employee questions about when and why the problem is occurring

2. Use straightforward, open-ended questions to find out what the employee thinks about the problem

3. Ask a series of questions about why the problem is occurring

4. With another manager, generate as many ideas as possible about reasons for the problem

5. Ask as many of the employee's colleagues as possible for their perceptions of the problem

6. Avoid discussion with the employee until you've reached a decision about the problem's cause

Answer

Option 1: This option is correct. It's important to involve the employee in diagnosing the problem's cause.

Option 2: This is a correct option. You should use simple, open-ended questions to find out what the employee knows and thinks about the performance problem.

Option 3: This is a correct option. A useful diagnostic technique is known as the five whys. It involves using a series of "why" questions to drill down to the root cause of the problem.

Option 4: This is a correct option. Brainstorming is a good technique for generating ideas about the possible root causes of a performance problem.

Option 5: This option is incorrect. You should be discreet about employee performance problems, limiting your questioning only to employees who are directly involved or affected.

Option 6: This is an incorrect option. It's important to involve the employee in diagnosing the cause of the problem. This person is often the best source of information about the problem.

IDENTIFYING PROBLEM CAUSES

Identifying problem causes

Your ultimate goal in diagnosing the root causes of performance problems is to find appropriate solutions. So it can help to ask what you or your organization can do, and what the relevant employee can do, to address a particular problem. A performance problem can have external causes, internal causes, or both.

External causes

External causes of performance problems come from the conditions or context in which an employee works, rather than being intrinsic to the employee.

Internal causes

Internal causes of performance problems lie with the relevant employees. Examples include low motivation and a lack of required skills.

It's best always to look for external causes of performance problems before assuming internal ones. This can help you overcome bias – and make it more likely that your diagnosis will be accurate.

Performance problems can have many types of external causes. For example, in investigating a problem, you should ask these questions:

- Did external pressures and competing priorities – such as conflicting schedules and deadlines – play a role?
- Did the employee have access to required resources and equipment?
- Was the employee appropriately assigned, with the right skills and knowledge, to complete the given tasks?
- Was the employee given suitable guidance and support?
- Was the employee given needed information, including any changes to requirements?

Evironmental conditions such as bad lighting, inadequate ventilation, noise, and poorly placed equipment can also all contribute to poor employee performance. You might determine whether any of these factors affected an employee's performance simply by asking whether the employee finds the current office setup comfortable.

Similarly, the actions or inactions of others can affect performance. For example, annoying behavior such as talking loudly on the telephone, raucous laughter, and noisy shuffling of papers can be a constant distraction for an employee at work.

Bureaucratic processes that lead to ineffective ways of working and that stifle individual creativity may also inhibit good performance.

Two additional external factors that can contribute to poor performance are ill-placed punishments and ill-placed rewards. Ill-placed punishments penalize employees for behavior that's actually appropriate, whereas ill-placed rewards are unintentional rewards for undesirable performance.

Ill-placed punishment occurs when, for example, colleagues mock a group of workers who must don company-required protective gear. An example of ill-placed rewards can happen when managers praise a reduction in service call times that resulted only because an important part of the process is routinely disregarded during servicing.

Question

Employees at a manufacturing company know that following safety guidelines during production is time consuming and may put the company's output numbers at risk. Adherence to some of the safety guidelines is therefore quietly discouraged. Rewards, such as employee bonuses, are given only for production-related achievements.

What is this an example of?

Options:

1. Ill-placed punishment
2. Ill-placed reward

Answer

In this example, employees are penalized if they perform in the desired way, rather than rewarded for behavior that's undesirable.

Internal causes of poor performance can relate to an individual employee's understanding, abilities, skills, attitude, motivation, and personal priorities.

Understanding

Employees may misunderstand what their core job responsibilities are or their roles in a company. They may also misunderstand what's required of them in relation to specific tasks.

So when you diagnose a performance problem, you should investigate whether it arose as a result of misunderstanding.

Abilities

An employee may lack the physical or mental capacity to perform particular jobs well. So you should ask whether the employee has the necessary abilities, including physical and mental potential, for the job.

Skills

Employees may require particular skills to perform well in their jobs. A skill is a particular competence or ability to apply knowledge to achieve a result. A skill can be learned, but only if the ability to learn it is there.

Examples of questions to ask are "Does the employee have the required skills?" and "Does this employee have the ability to acquire the needed skills?"

Attitude

An employee's attitude can lead to negativity or insubordination, which undermine authority and interfere with efforts to promote good performance. Insubordination may involve malicious gossip or going over a manager's head to someone more senior.

When diagnosing a performance problem, you should ask whether the employee has a bad attitude and, if so, whether this has an effect on other staff.

Motivation

Employees may find their jobs boring or lose interest in them over time.

Questions to ask in this regard are "Does the employee find the job stimulating?" and "Does the employee's job need to be redesigned?"

Personal priorities

Employees' personal priorities might prevent them from performing in the desired ways. For example, employees might focus on work that will help them acquire particular skills and be inattentive to their other duties.

Relevant questions to ask are "Is this employee focused on work?" and "Are the employee's priorities aligned with the department and the organization's priorities?"

Often if you solve an external cause of a performance problem, you'll inadvertently solve an internal cause too. That's why it's best to address external causes first. For example, an employee's misunderstanding of an assignment may stem from a lack of information.

A lack of skill may be the result of poor training or guidance, or reflect an inappropriate assignment of the employee. A lack of motivation may come from ill-placed punishment or rewards, or poor environmental conditions. Inappropriate priorities can come from a lack of information or from ill-placed punishment or rewards.

Other internal causes, such as a lack of commitment or ability, may be more difficult to solve. Resolving internal causes of problems often means having to change behaviors or attitudes, which can be challenging. It usually falls to the relevant employee to change. If the person isn't willing to change, it may require disciplinary measures.

Question

Which three examples of questions should you consider asking first when diagnosing an employee's performance problem?

Options:

1. Are there conflicting demands on the employee's time?

2. Does the employee have access to needed equipment?

3. Was the employee given enough details about what to do and how?

4. Is the physical or mental potential of the employee strong enough?

5. Does this employee have a bad attitude?

Answer

Option 1: This option is correct. This question investigates whether conflicting demands on the employee's time were a relevant external cause of the problem.

Option 2: This is a correct option. This question investigates the possible external cause of inadequate access to resources or equipment, so it's appropriate to ask it early on in the diagnostic process.

Option 3: This option is correct. This question is an appropriate one to ask early in the process because it checks for a possible external cause of the problem.

Option 4: This is an incorrect option. This question relates to a possible internal cause of the problem and so should be left for after you've investigated external causes.

Option 5: This option is incorrect. This question relates to a possible internal cause of the problem. You should ask it only after investigating possible external causes.

EVALUATING PROBLEM DIAGNOSES

Evaluating problem diagnoses

A final guideline for diagnosing performance problems is ensuring that the conclusions you draw are focused, complete, coherent, and impartial.

First it's vital to ensure that the information you've gathered about the problem is focused and complete. In other words, all the information should be directly relevant and you should check that nothing has been omitted.

For example, an employee doesn't understand a particular task and struggles to complete it. Ask questions to find out all the information that relates directly to that particular task. Avoid asking questions about tasks the employee does well.

To guide you when developing focused and complete information, ensure you try to answer the five questions about the problem. Remember not all questions about a problem will always be answered.

What?

You ask "what?" to define the problem. For example, you may ask "What seems to be causing constant miscalculations on customer quotes?"

Where?

You ask "where?" to help determine where the problem is occurring. For example, you could ask "Where are errors in customer quotes being made?"

When?

You ask "when?" to determine the time frame of the problem, as in "Does the problem occur only at certain times or is it constant?

Who?

You ask "who?" to determine who is involved in the problem. For example, you might identify one employee as being responsible for issuing customer quotes that include errors.

Why?

You ask "why?" to help determine the root cause of the problem. For example, the employee responsible for errors on customer quotes battles to read the numbers off a price list because the print is too small, which causes errors.

For the diagnosis of a problem to be coherent, you have to establish a clear link between the cause of the problem and the problem itself. For example, an employee isn't performing well because the employee isn't receiving market-related pay and feels unappreciated. The problem is the underperformance and the cause is underpayment.

Finally, your diagnosis must be impartial. Impartial means that emotions or hunches are not involved. For example, a manager accuses an employee of leaking company information because the manager doesn't trust that particular employee for no good reason. This is based on a bias.

However, if the same manager treats employees the same and asks all of them about how information may have leaked about the company, this would be impartial and not based on bias. By keeping your diagnosis focused, complete, coherent, and impartial, you should be able to determine whether a performance problem is a result of internal or external causes, or both.

For example, external causes can include poor ventilation in the office or unnecessary administration forms that slow down employee performance. Or in the case of internal causes, an employee just does not possess the right skills to perform a job properly.

Steps can then be taken to resolve the problem. This might involve the manager in charge, the relevant employee, or – in the case of a systemic change – the organization as a whole.

Case Study: Question 1 of 3
Scenario

Adam, a manager in a shipping company, is currently diagnosing the poor performance of Samuel, who's an employee on this team.

Question

What did Adam do right when diagnosing the causes of Samuel's poor performance?

Options:

1. He involved Samuel in the diagnostic process
2. He continued asking why the problem was occurring
3. He investigated external causes before assuming internal ones 4. He consulted Samuel's coworker

Answer

Option 1: This option is incorrect. Adam made the mistake of failing to discuss the problem with Samuel, who may have given him more accurate information.

Option 2: This is a correct option. Adam continued asking "why" questions in an attempt to drill down to the root cause of Samuel's performance problems.

Option 3: This option is correct. Adam was right to investigate possible external causes of the problem before assuming internal ones, like sloppiness or laziness on Samuel's part.

Option 4: This is an incorrect option. Adam should have consulted Samuel about the problem, rather than starting by speaking to one of his coworkers about it.

Case Study: Question 2 of 3

Which statements about the process Adam used to diagnose the causes of Samuel's performance problem are correct?

Options:

1. Adam considered only relevant information when investigating the problem

2. Adam identified a cause with a clear connection to the problem

3. Adam's diagnosis of the problem took all relevant information into account

4. Adam didn't allow the plausibility trap to cloud his judgment about the performance problem

5. Adam was subject to attributional bias

Answer

Option 1: This option is correct. Adam didn't factor irrelevant information into his assessment of the problem.

Option 2: This is a correct option. Adam's causal attribution was coherent. In other words, it made logical sense that an e-mail problem could have prevented Samuel from attending meetings or getting there on time.

Option 3: This option is incorrect. Adam failed to consult Samuel about the problem. He also didn't confirm that his conclusion was correct. So his diagnosis wasn't based on complete information.

Option 4: This is an incorrect option. Adam stuck to the first plausible cause of Samuel's poor performance and didn't waver from it or try find out more information. This meant he was subject to the plausibility trap.

Option 5: This option is incorrect. Attributional bias, which would have involved blaming Samuel – rather than investigating external causes – for the problem, didn't apply to Adam.

Case Study: Question 3 of 3

What can you conclude about the situation given Adam's actions?

Options:

1. Samuel may continue failing to attend meetings on time – or at all – for reasons Adam failed to uncover

2. Adam has resolved the performance problem by addressing its external causes

3. Adam can assume that Samuel will always come to him when he has serious work-related problems

Answer

Option 1: This is the correct option. Because Adam didn't involve Samuel in diagnosing the performance problem, he may have overlooked important causes of Samuel's behavior.

Option 2: This is an incorrect option. Adam can now reasonably expect Samuel to receive e-mails about the meetings, but he hasn't ensured that other factors aren't contributing to the performance problem. So he might not have fully resolved the problem.

Option 3: This option is incorrect. Samuel wasn't made aware of his performance problem or that it had been fixed. So Adam's actions won't make it more likely that Samuel will consult him about problems he experiences.

Adam focused only on relevant information about why Samuel was defaulting at meetings. He also searched for external causes first and found e-mails to be an external cause. However, he did fall victim to the plausibility trap − he didn't think about any other factors that could be contributing to Samuel's poor performance. Adam also failed to involve Samuel in the process of finding the cause of the problem.

CHAPTER 2 - FIRST STEPS FOR TURNING AROUND A PERFORMANCE PROBLEM

CHAPTER 2 - First Steps for Turning Around a Performance Problem

SECTION 1 - LEVELS OF PROBLEM PERFORMANCE AND INTERVENTION

SECTION 1 - Levels of Problem Performance and Intervention

Dealing with minor to moderate performance issues as they arise helps protect an organization's bottom line, prevents minor issues from developing into more serious problems, prevents surprises for managers and employees, and enhances employee morale.

Typically, single incidents and emerging patterns of poor performance can be handled informally, whereas persistent patterns should be handled through formal feedback. Disciplinary issues require formal action in line with organizational protocols.

PERFORMANCE MANAGEMENT VERSUS DISCIPLINE

Performance management versus discipline

As a leader, you're responsible for how well employees perform. So when an employee performs poorly, you need to recognize how bad the problem is and develop the most appropriate solution. Minor to moderate performance issues don't require formal actions or disciplinary procedures. You can usually address them informally, discussing the issues and clarifying expectations.

Single incidents of poor performance often fall into this category. Examples are an employee forgetting to complete a routine task, making a mistake in a report, or giving the wrong information to a colleague or customer.

Emerging patterns of poor performance may also qualify as mild to moderate issues. An example is an employee arriving at work 20 minutes late, two or three times in a week. More serious performance issues require formal disciplinary action. Problems at this level include mandated issues and persistent problem performance.

Mandated issues

Mandated issues are those outlined in company policy as requiring formal disciplinary action. Examples could include breaching medical privacy laws, sexual harassment, flaunting safety measures, or stealing.

Persistent problem performance

Persistent problem performance often arises when managers fail to address poor performance early on. The problematic behavior then becomes the norm. But even with early informal interventions, poor performance sometimes persists because employees are unwilling or unable to improve their behavior.

Examples of persistent problem performance are regular failure to meet deadlines, ongoing rudeness to coworkers, and frequent lateness. It's important to address these types of problems using formal interventions.

Managing employees' performance isn't about punishing poor performance. Instead it's about identifying causes and solving problems to prevent poor performance in the future. Managing minor to moderate performance problems as they arise reduces the need for formal disciplinary action.

BENEFITS OF MANAGING PERFORMANCE

Benefits of managing performance

Benefits of dealing effectively with minor performance problems are that this protects the bottom line for an organization, prevents minor issues from developing into more serious problems, prevents surprises for managers and employees, and enhances staff morale.

Protects the bottom line

Early interventions for poor performance directly lower company costs. Fewer people are fired for poor performance, and fewer people choose to leave because morale is better. This reduces the need to spend money on recruiting and training new employees.

Also, when your employees know you care about their work and want to help them get it right, they're more motivated to perform well. This contributes to an organization's overall success and profitability.

Prevents more serious problems

Early interventions prevent problems from becoming ingrained or habitual.

Addressing issues early may identify and prevent more serious underlying problems, which could taint a wider group of employees and cause more harm in the long run.

Prevents surprises

By identifying problems and clarifying expectations early, you ensure that both you and the relevant employees are aware of areas that need improvement.

For example, this prevents employees from being surprised by negative performance appraisals and ensures they have a chance to improve before formal interventions are required.

Enhances morale

If managers or supervisors deal with problems early, appropriately, and informally, employees are less likely to be afraid of admitting to making mistakes. They'll be less intimidated and more focused on performing well, and generally have better morale.

Also, coworkers often resent taking on additional work when someone isn't performing well. So addressing a problem early can help prevent tension and hostility among employees.

Question

What are the benefits of dealing with minor performance problems effectively?

Options:

1. It protects an organization's profitability

2. It helps prevent bigger problems

3. It ensures you and your employees aren't taken by surprise

4. It creates a more supportive and performance-oriented workplace, which boosts morale

5. It reduces the need for formal performance appraisals

6. It demonstrates that poor performance will be punished

Answer

Option 1: This option is correct. By catching and correcting problem performance early, you help protect an organization's bottom line by improving performance and reducing turnover.

Option 2: This option is correct. By addressing performance problems early, you help prevent problem behavior from becoming entrenched or more serious.

Option 3: This is a correct option. Identifying and addressing performance issues as they arise helps ensure managers and employees aren't taken by surprise – for example, by negative overall results or criticism delivered in formal performance appraisals.

Option 4: This option is correct. When minor problems are managed appropriately, employees feel less afraid of owning up to their mistakes, focus on performing well, and generally have better morale.

Option 5: This option is incorrect. Managing minor to moderate performance problems doesn't replace the need for formal performance appraisals.

Option 6: This is an incorrect option. Addressing minor performance issues early on doesn't involve punishing employees. It involves helping them identify and resolve the issues, and can help avoid the need for disciplinary action later on.

FORMAL AND INFORMAL INTERVENTIONS

Formal and informal interventions

It's important for managers to communicate regularly with employees about their performance – both formally and informally. Communication should occur through performance planning and formal appraisals, but also through regular feedback.

During regular feedback, you and the employees you manage should discuss what's working and what's not. This type of feedback increases collaboration and communication, ultimately improving performance and morale. The feedback you give may be formal or informal, depending on the situation.

Formal

Formal feedback may be given during disciplinary interventions, formal meetings, and formal performance appraisals. This type of feedback is documented and added to an employee's file. It's also expected that the feedback will comply with organizational protocols, such as the protocol for written warnings.

This type of feedback is most suitable for handling persistent problems or serious violations of company policy.

Informal

Informal communication includes casual conversations and counseling. These may be documented in a manager's records but aren't added to employees' files.

Organizational policy doesn't prescribe the content of these discussions. When feedback is about a performance problem, it's typical to describe the problem, determine why it's happening, and discuss potential solutions.

Hilary is one of the employees on the team you manage. Her verbal communications seem fine, but you've noticed that her memos and e-mails are littered with spelling and grammatical mistakes.

You take her aside and outline the problem. She agrees always to run a spell check on material she writes, and you both plan for her to take an English business grammar course at a night school to correct the problem.

This is an informal feedback session and you document it in your own files only.

Now suppose you overhear an employee, Adam, make an overtly sexist comment to a customer. This behavior is unacceptable and against company policy. You speak to personnel in the Human Resources Department and bring Adam in to give him a formal verbal warning about his behavior.

Because this intervention is formal, it should be documented and added to Adam's employee file.

Question

Classify examples of interventions associated with managing employee performance based on their type. More than one example may match to a type.

Options:

A. A written warning about persistent lateness

B. An annual performance appraisal

C. A casual discussion about ensuring that an employee uses updated pricing tables when providing quotes

D. A conversation with an employee about his lack of accuracy in internal reports

Targets:

1. Formal

2. Informal

Answer

Formal feedback is documented and added to an employee's file. Examples are the feedback in written warnings and annual performance appraisals.

Informal feedback includes casual discussions and counseling about mild to moderate performance issues, such as using the incorrect information or making minor mistakes in reports.

LEVELS OF INTERVENTION

Levels of intervention

Sometimes it can be tricky to decide what level of intervention a performance problem warrants. To help you do this, you can categorize a performance problem into one of five categories – a single incident that has been self-corrected, a single incident not yet corrected, an emerging pattern, a persistent pattern, or a disciplinary issue.

Single incident self-corrected

If an employee makes a mistake, notices the mistake, and tries to correct it, it's best to have an informal conversation. For example, this applies if an employee tells an inappropriate joke or snaps at someone in a meeting, and then immediately apologizes.

In these cases, it's sufficient to affirm that the behavior wasn't appropriate, to note that the mistake was corrected, and to gain a commitment that it won't happen again.

Single incident not yet corrected

If an employee makes a single mistake and hasn't corrected it yet, the issue needs to be handled informally and possible solutions should be discussed.

For example, if an employee is running behind schedule and hasn't informed those who may be affected by the delay, you need to explain why this behavior is a problem and discuss how it can be prevented in the future.

Emerging pattern

If an emerging pattern of poor performance arises because of an employee's lack of awareness, or a supervisor's failure to intervene earlier, it's best handled through informal conversation and a discussion of potential solutions.

For example, if an employee isn't keeping up to date with changes in technology in her field, you can explain why it's important to do so and discuss potential solutions, such as giving her more time for research or additional skills training.

Persistent pattern

If a persistent pattern of poor performance occurs due to an employee's lack of awareness, skill, or motivation, you should use a formal intervention to address the problem.

For example, if an employee is consistently late for work and meetings, and has used more than his allocation of sick days, you need to have a formal meeting. You should explain that this behavior will be recorded in his employee file and that it must stop immediately, or disciplinary action will be taken.

Disciplinary issue

Disciplinary issues are problems that need to be addressed through disciplinary action, because of their seriousness or because an employee's performance hasn't improved despite previous interventions.

For example, an employee who continues arriving at work over an hour late, after you've already discussed the issue, should be subject to formal disciplinary action.

Violations of company policies or mandates always require formal intervention in line with protocols laid out in organizational policy. These may be relatively minor issues, like violating a company's security protocol by failing to lock a door, or very serious issues – like releasing highly confidential information or physically assaulting another employee.

Question

Match each category of performance problem to the appropriate type of intervention. More than one category may match to each type of intervention.

Options:

A. Single incident, self-corrected
B. Single incident, not yet corrected
C. Emerging pattern
D. Persistent pattern
E. Disciplinary issue

Targets:

1. Informal conversation
2. Formal communication
3. Formal action

Answer

Informal conversations are sufficient for single-incident events and emerging patterns. If an incident hasn't yet been corrected or if a pattern is emerging, you need to discuss potential solutions.

Formal communication is required for persistent patterns of behavior due to lack of awareness, intervention, skill, or motivation.

Disciplinary issues require formal actions such as written warnings, suspensions, or terminations.

So casual communication or feedback is called for if you're intervening early and a problem is relatively minor. Formal communication is required when you're intervening late and a problem is persistent or critical.

Question

Suppose you've recently joined a company where you manage a team of business analysts. You notice a high number of customer complaints relating to Janice's rudeness and poor presentation skills. According to records in her employee file, the first incident was reported a year ago. Also, other team members complain that Janice is frequently rude and unhelpful. Janice's previous manager didn't address this with Janice.

How should you address this issue?

Options:

1. Hold a formal meeting with Janice explaining that this behavior is unacceptable, and set up a performance plan that she must keep to

2. Give Janice a formal written warning and discuss plans for how she can change this behavior

3. Chat with Janice about why she's performing badly and explore how she can change this behavior

Answer

Option 1: This is the correct option. Janice shows a persistent pattern of poor performance, so the best approach here is to use a formal intervention in the form of a meeting. Disciplinary action isn't warranted yet because her previous manager didn't address Janice's behavior. However, it will be warranted if Janice's performance doesn't improve after the meeting.

Option 2: This option is incorrect. Although Janice's performance problems are serious, no one has addressed the issue with her before. So her performance falls into the category of a persistent pattern, which should be addressed formally before you institute disciplinary action.

Option 3: This option is incorrect. Janice's poor performance is part of a persistent pattern of behavior, so it should be dealt with formally rather than informally.

SECTION 2 - STEPS TO COMMUNICATE PERFORMANCE ISSUES

SECTION 2 - Steps to Communicate Performance Issues

To give an employee effective feedback about a performance problem, you can follow a five-step process. You describe the issue, describe expectations for performance, determine what's causing the problem, generate solutions, and finally agree on solutions.

Understanding the problem

Knowing how to give effective feedback makes it easier to address performance problems. To ensure your feedback is effective, you can follow five steps. You describe the issue, describe expectations, determine the cause of the problem, generate solutions, and finally agree on solutions. This process should be handled in private, unless circumstances call for human resources personnel or other parties to be present.

Catherine is Ed's manager at a small software development company. She's noticed that Ed often arrives late, spends half an hour or longer after he arrives talking to people and making coffee, and sometimes leaves work early.

To address the issue, Catherine asks Ed to meet her in her office. As the first step, she then needs to describe the issue that's affecting Ed's performance.

When describing a problem to an employee, it's important that you follow certain guidelines. You need to stick to the actual performance issue and avoid jumping to any conclusions about why it's happening. It's also important to be specific, rather than speaking generally about the problem.

Stick to the issue

Catherine should focus only on Ed's lateness and poor timekeeping, or she'll dilute her message about the problem.

She also needs to avoid making assumptions about the reasons for Ed's poor performance. For example, Catherine may be tempted to accuse Ed of showing poor effort. However, she doesn't yet know what's causing the problem.

Be specific

Catherine needs to list incidents of the problem behaviors and the results of these. She should also be specific about exactly when each of these incidents occurred.

For example, it's not effective for Catherine just to say something general like "You're not sticking to your agreed work hours and this has a negative impact." Instead, she should say something specific, like "You arrived late on Monday and Wednesday, and left work early on Thursday. Once you arrive, you don't sit down at your desk for the first 30 minutes or so. This behavior disrupts other employees' work and gives the impression that it's not necessary to keep to working hours."

The next step for Catherine is to describe the expected standards of employee performance to Ed. Follow along as she does this.

Catherine: Ed, do you know your official work hours?

Ed: Yes. I know the official times are 9:00 a.m. to 5:00 p.m., but we often work overtime and take work home – so I feel the hours are more of a guideline than a rule.

Catherine: I understand everyone has been working hard lately, but your contract specifies that your working day begins at 9:00 a.m. and runs to 5:00 p.m. We need to keep to this. That way, when coworkers need to collaborate with you, they know when you'll be around.

When describing the expectations of employee performance, Catherine does quite a good job. She's specific about times and expectations. She also states where these expectations are documented. She avoids overly general statements such as "we expect more of you" or "we expect you to be on time."

Once you've described the problem and outlined expectations, you need to ask questions to help you determine the cause of the problem. This isn't an opportunity to criticize the employee, but to explore the root causes of the problem and prevent it from reoccurring. So at this stage, you should be careful to avoid assigning blame.

Often problems that seem to be the fault of an individual turn out to be the result of circumstances that have nothing to do with the individual's attitude, abilities, or personal circumstances. So it's important not to assume that whenever there's a performance problem, the cause lies with the employee. Instead, you should search for possible external causes.

Your list of potential external causes of performance problems may have included some common issues:

external pressures and competing priorities – such as tight schedules, unreasonable deadlines, and pressure from coworkers,

inadequate resources or equipment – for example, missing software or outdated equipment,

inappropriate assignments, with employees given tasks they shouldn't reasonably be expected to perform and aren't equipped to complete properly,

poor guidance or support from managers or team members,

lack of information, such as incomplete instructions for performing a task correctly,

poor environmental conditions, such as poor lighting, uncomfortable work spaces, or poor placement of equipment, and

the actions or inactions of others, such as excessive bureaucracy.

Inappropriate punishment and rewards are also external factors that can lead to poor employee performance. For example, good performance is punished if employees who manage difficult assignments are singled out and continually given the most difficult work. Poor performance is rewarded if latecomers to meetings never have to wait for the meetings to commence – whereas the punctual people are forced to wait.

Sometimes the causes of performance problems do lie with the relevant employees. So after ruling out all external causes, you should investigate a range of possible internal causes:

- lack of understanding, for example of guidelines or of a required process,

- lack of ability or of the skills needed to perform a given task,
- inappropriate attitude, such as lack of respect for coworkers or authority, or an unreasonable sense of entitlement,
- poor motivation, for example demonstrated through a lack of interest or an unwillingness to complete a task, or
- inappropriate personal priorities, such as prioritizing office relationships or making personal phone calls at the expense of work.

Keeping these potential causes in mind, Catherine could ask Ed something like "What's making it difficult for you to be punctual?" She should avoid jumping to conclusions or asking questions that demonstrate unfair judgments, like "Why do you think you can get away with doing less than everyone else?"

GENERATING A SOLUTION

Generating a solution

Once you've established the causes of problem performance, you can begin to generate potential solutions. But it's unlikely you'll get an employee's full commitment to overcoming a problem if you just decide what's required and then tell this person what to do. Instead, you should collaborate. So you should first ask the employee for suggestions on what may solve the issue. Then jointly discuss potential solutions. And finally, select solutions you both agree on.

1. Ask for suggestions

It's important to first ask the employee to suggest solutions before you offer ideas of your own. You may not even need to follow up with your own suggestions.

Say Catherine determines that overwork combined with poor time management is causing Ed's lack of punctuality. She should ask Ed what he thinks could solve the problem. She shouldn't begin the conversation by offering what she thinks will work.

2. Jointly discuss solutions

Once you have a set of potential solutions, you need to discuss and refine them jointly. In some cases, discussion may lead to improvements to suggested solutions.

For example, Catherine thinks that improving Ed's time management skills and delegating some of his work to others are useful ideas. Ed thinks that reassigning some of his tasks and allowing him to telecommute two days per week are viable options. All these suggestions should be discussed and refined.

3. Select solutions

The final step is to select solutions that both you and the employee agree are the best.

For example, Catherine and Ed agree that Ed will complete a one-hour course on time management and that Catherine will reassign some of Ed's research work. Ed's more likely to commit to overcoming the problem because he agrees to both these measures.

Question

Which statements or questions are appropriate when communicating with an employee about a performance problem?

Options:

1. "Your sales figures have dropped from 75 to 30, and our minimum expectation is 40."

2. "Your output has been disappointing and I expect more of you."

3. "You don't seem to care about the quality of your work or you wouldn't be making so many errors."

4. "Is there a problem with the equipment or your colleagues that's contributing to the problem?"

5. "What do you think would help solve this problem?"

6. "I think that setting up your workstation so you can easily reach your tools could help. What do you think?"

Answer

Option 1: This option is correct. This statement identifies the problem, which is low sales figures, in relation to the expectation that the employee should be meeting.

Option 2: This option is incorrect. Saying that output is disappointing and more is expected is too vague. Output and expectations should be quantified.

Option 3: This option is incorrect. Saying that someone doesn't care about the quality of the work is inappropriate because it makes assumptions about why the problem is occurring and puts the blame on the employee.

Option 4: This is a correct option. Asking whether equipment or colleagues are the causes of the problem is useful because these are possible external causes. You should search for external causes before establishing whether the causes lie with the employee.

Option 5: This is a correct option. When generating solutions, it's important to ask employees for their suggestions rather than being prescriptive.

Option 6: This option is correct. It's important to discuss possible solutions with the employee, inviting this person's opinions rather than being prescriptive.

The last step is to agree on specific solutions and when to implement them. You should also plan to meet again to check on progress and results. So for example, Ed agrees to complete the time management course – which is available on the intranet – by the end of the day. Catherine also agrees to reassign some of his research tasks by the following morning.

Although informal conversations aren't officially documented, you need to use your notes to guide you during the follow-up. For instance, Catherine writes the agreed solutions and deadlines in her task list and goes through them with Ed the following morning.

Question

Sequence examples of the steps in the process of communicating with an employee about a performance problem.

Options:

A. Specify that the employee was rude to someone from the Accounting Department that morning B. State that employees are expected to treat one another with respect

C. Ask why the employee behaved in the way he did

D. Ask what the employee thinks would help reduce the stress of collecting data by deadlines

E. Confirm that the employee agrees to request needed data a day in advance, via e-mail

Answer

Specify that the employee was rude to someone from the Accounting Department that morning is ranked the first step. The first step in the process is to describe the issue or problem performance – in this case, disrespectful behavior toward a colleague.

State that employees are expected to treat one another with respect is ranked the second step. The second step is to describe the expectations of the organization and to specify where these expectations are documented.

Ask why the employee behaved in the way he did is ranked the third step. The third step is to determine the cause of the problem behavior. Typically, you should look for external causes before considering potential internal causes.

Ask what the employee thinks would help reduce the stress of collecting data by deadlines is ranked the fourth step. The fourth step is to generate solutions. In this step, you should begin by asking the employee for suggestions.

Confirm that the employee agrees to request needed data a day in advance, via e- mail is ranked the fifth step. The fifth step is agreeing on specific actions to take and when to take them.

SECTION 3 - COMMUNICATING ABOUT PROBLEM PERFORMANCE

SECTION 3 - Communicating About Problem Performance

When addressing an employee's minor to moderate performance problem, it's important to follow five steps for giving effective feedback. It's also important not to apologize for addressing the problem, not to enter into arguments about other employees, and not to be manipulated by the employee's emotions.

FOLLOWING THE PROCESS

Following the process

You're likely to encounter emotional responses when communicating with employees about problem performance. To help you through this, you should avoid apologizing, avoid arguments about other employees, and avoid being manipulated.

Apologizing

It's your job to monitor and improve employees' performance, so don't apologize for communicating about the problem. However, it's important to stay curious, neutral, and supportive. This will encourage the employee to discuss the issue honestly and openly.

Arguments about others

Don't get drawn into an argument. For example, if an employee says she can't meet deadlines because she has to wait for information from someone else, focus on what measures could ensure she gets information on time and what she can do while waiting for information.

If the complaint is a serious one, speak to coworkers and others to find out the full story before deciding how to proceed.

Being manipulated

Employees may become emotional when discussing performance problems. Showing too much sympathy may derail the conversation.

Generally, it's best to keep tissues in the office. If employees start to cry, calmly give them the tissues, and when they've regained control, continue the conversation where you left off.

This approach acknowledges the emotion without engaging with it and it provides employees with time to regain control.

SECTION 4 - RESOLVING THE PROBLEM

SECTION 4 - Resolving the Problem

Some performance issues can be addressed quickly and easily through fast fixes. These include clarifying expectations, providing needed information, providing resources, or providing feedback and support about performance issues.

For more complex performance issues, you can use longer-term strategies such as skills development and redefining work. These are useful when an employee lacks the required skills or ability. The employee in these cases should be responsible for agreeing to training, making more effort, or having a coach or mentor.

When the cause of a problem lies with employee motivation or attitude, you can use appropriate rewards, set clear consequences, and encourage self-monitoring. You can suggest an employee assistance program if the problem is personal. Employee responsibilities include agreeing to put in the needed effort, self-monitoring, or agreeing to coaching.

FAST FIXES

Fast fixes

After you communicate with employees about performance problems, you may have discovered that it's possible to take immediate steps to help resolve the problems. A range of fast fixes may be appropriate. These are solutions that are easily within your authority and capacity to implement, and that don't require widespread change or effort. Common fast fixes include clarifying expectations, providing information, providing resources, and providing feedback and support.

Clarifying expectations

You should describe the expectations an employee should be meeting when you first notice and communicate a problem. However, sometimes the employee may not understand or be clear about some of the unspoken rules or nuances related to accountability and chains of responsibility. It's important to clarify these.

A useful technique when clarifying expectations one-on-one is to ask the employee to explain the expectations back to you, to ensure they've been fully understood.

Providing information

Sometimes employees simply don't have the information needed to perform the tasks they're assigned correctly.

For example, an employee may not know where to find the latest figures for inclusion in a report, or who to call when there's a technical problem. Or an employee might not be given important background information about clients.

To provide information to facilitate performance, you can use regular staff meetings, e-mails, discussions, in-house refresher courses, and procedure manuals.

Providing resources

Sometimes you can easily address performance problems by providing employees with the appropriate resources.

For example, you should organize the purchase of software an employee may need to perform a task, or provide ergonomic tools such as a gel wrist rest mouse pad or an ergonomic keyboard for an administrative clerk who spends long hours capturing data.

Providing feedback and support

You need to provide feedback and support as a quick fix when employees aren't yet in a position to recognize good from bad performance. It's important that feedback is timely. Also, asking employees what they have understood from the feedback helps to ensure that they're clear about where they're performing well and where they need to improve.

For example, if a new hire in a call center doesn't greet a customer in an appropriately professional way, you can explain the problem and ask the employee for an example of how to greet the next customer who calls.

Question

Match fast fixes to problem situations that they could resolve.

Options:

A. Clarifying expectations

B. Providing information

C. Providing resources

D. Providing feedback and support

Targets:

1. A sales representative doesn't know that she's meant to close a minimum of ten sales a month

2. A teleworker doesn't know the address for the database in which to record the hours he works offsite

3. A trainer is unable to use a slide show as part of her presentation because the projector is broken

4. A purchaser is unaware that he treated a supplier disrespectfully

Answer

If the sales representative knows she's expected to close a certain number of sales per month, she can direct her efforts toward meeting this expectation.

If the teleworker is given information about where to find the database and how to use it, he'll be able to record his hours.

If the trainer is provided with the necessary resources – in this case, a functioning projector – her performance will improve.

If the employee is unaware of his poor performance when handling suppliers, he needs feedback about this and support in determining how to improve his performance.

DEVELOPMENT AND WORK DEFINITION

Development and work definition

If employees' performance problems persist after you've implemented fast fixes, you may need to resort to more complex solutions. It's important to determine these solutions in collaboration with the employees. This approach ensures buy-in from the employees and motivates better performance.

The solutions you and an employee develop should depend on the causes of a performance problem. These may become clear only over the course of several conversations and as you try to address the problem.

As causes become clearer, you can devise more specific solutions, ensuring they're viable for the employee and your organization.

Two important long-term solutions for minor-to-moderate performance problems are developing an employee's skills and knowledge, and redesigning work to suit the specific employees and resources that are available.

Developing skills and knowledge

If a lack of skill or knowledge is contributing to a performance problem, you can offer options such as web-based or classroom training, job shadowing, mentoring, and coaching.

Coaching is a technique that usually supplements and supports other skill development initiatives. It involves having an employee learn from someone more experienced. A good coach provides guidance but leaves employees to identify options and select their own ways of handling situations. For coaching to succeed, though, it has to be voluntary.

Redesigning work

If an employee lacks the underlying ability – rather than skill – to meet expectations, or major obstacles prevent this, you may need to redesign the employee's work. This can involve reassigning people to work better suited to them, adding staff to mitigate an overload, or streamlining processes.

For example, if an employee has good verbal skills but poor visual acuity, having that employee work out design issues is impractical. Similarly, an employee who already has a large workload may be unable to complete a further task by a given deadline.

Catherine is Ed's supervisor at a small software development company. In the process of discussing his poor timekeeping, she discovers that Ed is being given work that he's not trained for and is trying to complete tasks that two people managed previously. Follow along as Catherine and Ed discuss whether to develop Ed's skills or redefine the work.

Catherine: So you've been trying to learn the code while trying to keep to the deadline?

Ed: Yes. I've been working long hours at home. Then when I do get the coding right, I still have to come in and test it with the rest of the code. Finally, I have to implement fixes to my code and to the existing code.

Catherine: So there's simply too much work to do?

Ed: Yes. I suppose I could get through more if I had some formal training on this type of coding.

Catherine: I agree. Let's get you that training. But we also need to delegate some of the work to another employee. I can assign the code's lab testing to someone else so that it's no longer part of your job.

In their discussion, Catherine and Ed settle on both approaches. Ed agrees to training as a way to develop his skills, and Catherine agrees to redesign Ed's work – handing one of Ed's usual responsibilities to a different employee.

SUPPORT AND MOTIVATION

Support and motivation

If a lack of skills or ability are not the causes of performance problems, the solutions might involve increasing employees' motivation and providing personal support for employees.

It's appropriate to focus on increasing motivation when it's obvious that an employee is unwilling or reluctant to meet expectations.

Changing employees' attitudes can be difficult, so you typically begin by encouraging changes in behavior.

You can motivate employees to change their behavior by using rewards and setting clear consequences, for both desirable and undesirable performance. You can also get employees involved in monitoring their own performance through the use of built-in feedback.

Rewards

One way you can promote a desire to change behavior is by offering tailor-made rewards, based on what will motivate a particular individual. These rewards should be closely aligned with individual or team performance.

Some examples of rewards that can be offered for good performance are financial bonuses, recognition, increased responsibility, opportunities for development, and extra vacation days.

Consequences

It's important to link performance to clear consequences – with positive consequences for good performance and negative ones for poor performance.

If employees know they'll be held accountable for meeting expectations, but also that they'll be rewarded for doing well, they're more likely to be motivated.

Built-in feedback

Built-in feedback is feedback employees get about their performance in the course of doing their jobs. For instance, employees in a call center may monitor any complaints from the customers whose queries they handle. Examples of other sources of built-in feedback are activity reports, work logs, and customer or supplier feedback surveys.

Using built-in feedback helps ensure employees get regular information about their performance and know where they can improve. Because it involves them directly in monitoring and managing their own performance, it also typically boosts their motivation.

It's appropriate to provide personal support when an employee is dealing with personal problems and this affects the person's performance.

Personal issues that might affect employees' performance include substance abuse, emotional distress, family or relationship issues, and health-related, financial, or legal concerns.

As a manager, you should avoid inquiring about personal problems or attempting to counsel an employee yourself. Instead, suggest the employee visit a suitably qualified professional, via an employee assistance program if one is available.

An employee assistance program is a body that provides professional and confidential support to employees and their families.

This type of program may address issues such as addiction or coping with trauma. It's designed to help employees address personal issues affecting their performance.

Employee assistance programs are voluntary for employees, but employers can make them available and recommend their use.The benefits of these programs for organizations can include reducing absenteeism and insurance claims, and managers will be focusing on performance – rather than personal counseling, which is handled separately.

Suppose an employee appears to lack motivation and has a careless attitude to her work. In this case, you can use a combination of rewards, consequences, and built-in feedback to address the issue and improve the employee's motivation.

However, if the problem arises due to personal issues that distract the employee from performing well, you may recommend that she visit a professional via an employee assistance program. This involves providing personal support.

It's important that employees take some responsibility for turning their performance problems around. This can involve agreeing to change their behavior and attitudes, self-monitoring, and agreeing to coaching, or training.

Behavior and attitudes

When a lack of motivation or a poor attitude is the cause of poor performance, it's the employee's responsibility to agree to put in the effort needed to improve performance.

Self monitoring

Gaining a commitment from an employee to engage in active self-monitoring is a useful strategy when motivation or attitude is a root cause of the problem.

Coaching

If an employee's lack of motivation or skills is causing a performance problem, having the employee agreeing to be coached or mentored is a useful solution.

Training

If a lack of skills or knowledge is the cause of an employee's performance issue, a useful solution would be to get the employee to agree to complete some form of training.

Once you and an employee have agreed to the solutions and responsibilities, you should document the planned actions, time lines, and agreements for future reference.

Remember this doesn't constitute a formal write-up for the employee's file. It's simply meant to record what happened and to help you remember to follow up on the employee's progress, and discuss outcomes and subsequent requirements.

Follow-up should include regular feedback. Checking in and documenting improvement is also important. If performance should continue to decline, then you'll need records of your contribution and the employee's unsatisfactory response.

Question

Gerald, who's one of the employees you manage, has been producing low-quality work. When discussing this, you find that he feels demoralized because he hasn't been given team lead positions in various projects despite his formerly good work. You and Gerald are in the process of determining and agreeing on actions to take to turn the problem around.

Which are appropriate ways for you and Gerald to resolve the problem?

Options:

1. Let Gerald know that if his performance exceeds requirements, he'll be considered for the position of team lead for the next project

2. Redesign Gerald's work so that he focuses on tasks that he finds more enjoyable

3. Provide personal support and suggest Gerald make use of an employee assistance program to boost his self-confidence

4. Have Gerald agree to assess his own performance, noting areas where he can improve 5. Have Gerald agree to put in the effort needed to improve his skills

6. Have Gerald agree to complete training to improve his output

Answer

Option 1: This option is correct. The cause of the problem is Gerald's lack of motivation. One of the ways you can boost an employee's motivation is by offering a reward for good performance. This reward should be tailored for the individual.

Option 2: This is an incorrect option. Redesigning work is appropriate when an employee lacks the ability to carry out the work. Gerald lacks motivation, not ability.

Option 3: This option is incorrect. The scenario doesn't mention personal problems. Gerald lacks motivation for his work, so appropriate strategies include using rewards, setting clear consequences for good and bad performance, and encouraging Gerald to monitor his own performance.

Option 4: This option is correct. Having Gerald monitor his own performance will increase his sense of control and responsibility. In turn, this is likely to improve his motivation.

Option 5: This option is incorrect. Gerald has the needed skills – his work was good in the past. He requires strategies to build his motivation and needs to take responsibility for changing his actions.

Option 6: This is an incorrect option. The cause here is Gerald's lack of motivation, rather than a lack of skill that could be addressed through training.

CHAPTER 3 - USING PROGRESSIVE DISCIPLINE TO CORRECT PROBLEM PERFORMANCE

CHAPTER 3 - Using Progressive Discipline to Correct Problem Performance

SECTION 1 - WHEN TO USE PROGRESSIVE DISCIPLINE

SECTION 1 - When to Use Progressive Discipline

Progressive discipline involves imposing increasingly severe penalties on employees over time if their performance doesn't improve. The goal is to facilitate improvements before it becomes necessary to dismiss the employees.

Progressive discipline is appropriate when expectations and consequences have been clearly spelled out, the employee is aware of and able to meet the expectations, and there's a deliberate transgression of expectations with no extenuating circumstances. It's not appropriate if relevant work rules, policies, and performance standards haven't been clearly communicated or consistently enforced, there's insufficient evidence of the violation, or someone breaks the law.

PROGRESSIVE DISCIPLINE

Progressive discipline

Picture a snowball rolling down a hill. It gets bigger and more out of control the further it progresses. In the same way, employee performance problems can progress beyond minor issues into more serious, persistent ones.

Performance transgressions occur when employees fail to meet work-related expectations. An example is being consistently late in submitting a department's monthly figures to administration. A salesperson failing to meet a minimum, agreed sales target is another example.

Minor to moderate performance problems that result from situational factors, misunderstandings, and short-lived issues can be easily resolved. They call for "fast fixes" that the manager can implement, such as clarifying expectations, providing needed resources or information, or adjusting an employee's responsibilities or workload.

In other cases, performance problems are more troublesome even after the manager has communicated the problems to the relevant employees and tried to work with them to find solutions.

Progressive discipline is a suitable way to deal with persistent performance problems. It's a disciplinary process that holds employees accountable for the results they're expected to achieve. The process is described as progressive because continued failure to meet expectations is met with increasingly severe penalties over time. Ultimately, though, the goal of progressive discipline isn't to punish. It's to help employees improve before dismissal can be considered.

Discipline should be progressive when an employee repeats the same type of transgression after a manager has already communicated the problem. Note that this type of discipline isn't called for when an employee commits completely different types of transgressions at different times. In a case like this, each transgression would have to be addressed separately.

At each stage in the progressive discipline process, the aim is to work with the employee to outline steps to take to solve the performance problem.

Question

What do you think are benefits of using progressive discipline to address a performance problem?

Options:

1. It involves the employee

2. It demonstrates your commitment to employees

3. It enables you to defend your actions in a wrongful dismissal claim

4. It establishes a clear relationship between violations

5. It clearly demonstrates your authority

6. It encourages problematic employees to leave, making it unnecessary to fire them

Answer

Option 1: This is a correct option. At each stage in a progressive discipline process, the employee is given the chance to participate directly in addressing the relevant performance problem.

Option 2: This option is correct. By giving employees multiple opportunities to address performance problems – and by offering them your help in doing this – you indicate your commitment to them.

Option 3: This is a correct option. In cases where employees are eventually dismissed and file legal claims of unfair dismissal against your company, records of progressive discipline provide evidence that managers followed due process. They show that managers alerted the employees to problems and gave them multiple opportunities to improve before choosing to dismiss them.

Option 4: This option is correct. If you take progressively more severe disciplinary actions in response to repeated transgressions, it establishes a clear link between the transgressions. This can prompt an employee to take the need to improve more seriously.

Option 5: This option is incorrect. Although a manager needs to exercise authority during the progressive discipline process, this isn't a particular benefit or goal of the process.

Option 6: This option is incorrect. The goal of progressive discipline is to help an employee resolve a performance problem, rather than to intimidate this person into leaving.

So the benefits of progressive discipline are that it involves employees, demonstrates your commitment to supporting them, links similar transgressions, and protects your company in the case of legal claims of unfair dismissal.

Question

Which definition most accurately describes progressive discipline?

Options:

1. Progressive discipline is an incremental disciplinary process that's applied to employees who repeatedly fail to meet performance expectations

2. Progressive discipline is a process that punishes employees for failure to meet performance objectives

3. Progressive discipline is a process of working out suitable action plans for employees that aren't performing and monitoring their progress over time

Answer

Option 1: This is the correct option. Key elements of progressive discipline are clearly defined expectations and consequences, and penalties that carry increasing weight if performance failures continue.

Option 2: This is an incorrect option. Progressive discipline is a reasonable process with the primary motivation of rehabilitating, not punishing, the employee.

Option 3: This option is incorrect. Working out a suitable action plan and monitoring the employee's progress is only one part of progressive discipline.

WHEN TO APPLY PROGRESSIVE DISCIPLINE

When to apply progressive discipline

In a business context, the idea of due process refers to following a reasonable and clearly defined process to address issues. In relation to managing employees, it can be seen as the duty managers have to be fair when addressing performance problems. It protects employees against unfair disciplinary actions, including unfair dismissal.

For example, due process for addressing a performance problem includes letting employees know when and why their performance is unacceptable.

It includes giving them the opportunity to explain their actions.

And it involves giving them the chance to improve their performance before more drastic steps – like termination of employment – are taken.

As well as helping ensure you comply with employment laws, applying due process in your disciplinary actions is ethically responsible and makes good business sense. It can have several business advantages:

- it can help you uncover the real causes of a problem, which may lie with process or system flaws rather than being the fault of a particular employee,
- it's almost always cheaper to resolve a performance problem than to do nothing or to dismiss an experienced employee and recruit and train a replacement, and
- it can provide your organization with legal protection against wrongful discharge claims.

Following due process for addressing a performance problem includes ensuring the employee has an understanding of expectations and consequences, that management implements disciplinary actions with consistency, and that discipline is appropriate to the offense. It also involves giving the employee an opportunity to respond and a reasonable period of time to improve performance.

Expectations and consequences

A key element of following due process is ensuring the employee has a clear understanding of performance expectations and of the consequences for failing to meet these.

You should outline expectations when you hire someone or when expectations change. You should reiterate these expectations when you first detect a performance problem to assist the employee and to protect the interests of your organization.

Consistency

Sorin Dumitrascu

To uphold due process, managers need to be consistent in identifying specific behavior as problematic and in their responses to the behavior. For example, it's important to treat all employees fairly and without favoritism, and always impose the same penalties for particular transgressions.

You also need to be consistent in carrying out threats and implementing punishments, or you risk damaging the credibility of your disciplinary system.

Appropriate to offense

Due process depends on applying discipline that's appropriate and fair given the nature of the offense an employee has committed. For example, it's obviously inappropriate to dismiss an employee just for minor offenses and occasional poor performance.

You should also take an employee's performance track record and previous disciplinary history into account.

Opportunity to respond

To uphold due process, you need to give employees you accuse of failing to meet expectations the opportunity to respond and to defend their actions.

This can help prevent later disciplinary actions you take from being judged as arbitrary or unreasonable. In some cases, employees may alert you to factors outside their control that affected their performance.

Reasonable time to improve

To follow due process, you need to give an employee who's failing to meet expectations a reasonable period of time to make required performance improvements.

The time that's reasonable will depend on the problem. For example, you might expect an employee who's frequently absent to demonstrate improvement within two weeks. Another employee might need several months to acquire a missing skill.

Carefully following the sequence involved in progressive discipline, as well as the guidelines for when this approach is appropriate, is the best way to ensure you consistently uphold due process.

Progressive discipline is appropriate when three conditions are met: expectations and consequences have been clearly spelled out, the employee is aware of and able to meet the expectations, and there's a deliberate transgression of expectations with no extenuating circumstances.

Examples of types of problems that often warrant progressive discipline are excessive absenteeism, tardiness, insubordination, sabotage, and the failure to achieve specified results despite adequate training and resources.

Progressive discipline is not appropriate if the relevant work rules, policies, and performance standards haven't been clearly communicated or consistently enforced, or there's insufficient evidence of a violation. It's also not appropriate when someone breaks the law. If an employee does something illegal, it might be appropriate to terminate that person's employment immediately – and you may be required to report the issue to an external authority.

For example, progressive discipline would be appropriate in the case of an employee who deliberately and consistently ignores a company's clearly stated formal dress code. Conversely, progressive discipline would be inappropriate if an employee was caught stealing from petty cash. This is a criminal offense, so dismissal is the most appropriate response.

Question

Which conditions are necessary for applying progressive discipline?

Options:

1. A deliberate violation without extenuating circumstances has occurred

2. The employee is aware of expectations and of how to meet them, but fails to do so

3. There is sufficient evidence of a violation

4. The employee has broken the law

5. Relevant rules, policies, and standards haven't been consistently enforced

Answer

Option 1: This option is correct. Unless you can identify a special circumstance that makes the violation excusable, a deliberate infraction usually warrants progressive discipline.

Option 2: This option is correct. If guidelines and expectations for behavior are clear and available to the employee, failure to meet expectations usually warrants progressive discipline.

Option 3: This option is correct. Progressive discipline is a rational process that's only credible if there is clear evidence of a violation.

Option 4: This option is incorrect. Dismissal is the most appropriate response to illegal activity.

Option 5: This option is incorrect. For progressive discipline to follow due process, rules, policies, and standards need to be consistently enforced. If not, managers may be liable for charges of bias or discrimination.

Before choosing to implement progressive discipline, you should move through two key steps – provide positive discipline, and then monitor and check for performance improvement.

Provide positive discipline

You use positive discipline as an early step to hold employees accountable by talking about the problem with them. You then work together to diagnose the underlying root causes in order to identify and implement solutions. Typical solutions include clarifying expectations, providing information, and clearing obstacles to good performance.

Monitor and check

Once you've identified a solution and started to implement it, you need to monitor and check for performance improvement. You can do so by watching for performance indicators.

Positive performance indicators include completing the work on time, meeting quality or service standards, and carrying out the work as required. Negative performance indicators include failure to meet deadlines despite reminders, not following instructions, and showing little concern over the quality of the work produced.

If a problem persists after you've applied the two steps, it's time to begin the progressive discipline process – with "negative" discipline, or penalties, for failing to improve.

Consider Andrea. She works as the receptionist at Dr. Parker's practice. Dr. Parker isn't happy about Andrea's excessive use of the practice's phone for her personal calls. Technically, nothing in her contract or job description stipulates that she may not use the company's phone for personal use. He has, however, mentioned to her on a few occasions that she needs to limit the number of personal calls she makes from the office.

Is this an appropriate situation to begin progressive discipline? At first glance, it might seem that Dr. Parker engaged in positive discipline when he told Andrea that she should restrict her personal calls. However, during those conversations, he failed to work with Andrea to establish if there were any underlying causes and to identify possible solutions. He also didn't specify what her call limit should be.

So it isn't appropriate for Dr. Parker to implement progressive discipline. He first needs to communicate clearly with Andrea about the problem and to set up a system to monitor her subsequent performance.

Case Study: Question 1 of 2
Scenario

Dean arrives at work at exactly 8:30 a.m. every morning – the company's official start time. The problem is that everyone else arrives ten minutes early and is ready to begin work by this time, which is the company's expectation. Dean's colleagues complain that although Dean is theoretically on time for work, he only starts his day later – thereby preventing them from starting their work at 8:30 a.m. Angela, his manager, has mentioned to him that he should make more effort to begin work on time, but this has had little effect.

Help Angela determine whether this situation warrants progressive discipline by answering the questions in order.

Question

Is progressive discipline appropriate in this case?

Options:

1. Yes

2. No

Answer

Option 1: This option is incorrect. It would be premature to use progressive discipline in this case. Instead, Angela should begin by speaking to Dean about the problem less formally.

Option 2: This is the correct option. Before implementing a process of progressive discipline, Angela should communicate with Dean to identify what he could do to resolve the problem. She should implement progressive discipline only if this approach doesn't result in performance improvement.

Case Study: Question 2 of 2

Why is progressive discipline not appropriate in this case?

Options:

1. No positive disciplinary action has been taken

2. There's insufficient evidence of violations by Dean

3. It's clear that extenuating circumstances are driving Dean's behavior

4. The organization's policies, standards, and rules haven't been clearly communicated

5. Dean broke the law

Answer

Option 1: This option is correct. Although Angela casually told Dean not to be late for work, she didn't make the problem or relevant expectations about his performance clear. She also didn't invite a response from Dean or collaborate with him in deciding how to address the problem.

Option 2: This is a correct option. Technically, Dean arrives at work on time and there's no record that he's been failing to meet expectations surrounding his attendance at work.

Option 3: This option is incorrect. Because Angela failed to engage with Dean regarding the reasons for his arriving late to work and no subsequent meeting has been held since his latest offense, she has no way of knowing whether Dean's violations have been deliberate or if there are extenuating circumstances.

Option 4: This is a correct option. Angela didn't ensure Dean was familiar with the organization's expectations regarding his start time. Her failure to do so has severely hampered her options for dealing with the situation now. She needs to start from the beginning, using positive discipline and communicating the necessary information.

Option 5: This option is incorrect. There's no indication that Dean has broken the law – but if he had, it would be inappropriate to implement progressive discipline.

SECTION 2 - GIVING A VERBAL WARNING

SECTION - Giving a Verbal Warning

To uphold due process when addressing persistent performance problems, it's important that you follow a process of progressive discipline. This process includes three stages – giving a verbal warning, giving an initial written warning, and giving a final written warning.

To deliver an effective verbal warning, you need to begin with a clear statement of the problem and end by stating what will happen if specific improvement doesn't take place within a given time. You should focus on the problem without making it personal, stifling the employee's motivation, or attributing problems to the employee's state of mind. You should give the employee an opportunity to talk and ask questions, and you should remain firm and in control of the discussion.

STAGES OF PROGRESSIVE DISCIPLINE

Stages of progressive discipline

If an employee's poor performance continues after a manager has used an informal approach to address it, it's time to conduct a more formal process. You can uphold due process by following the sequence of the progressive discipline process and its associated guidelines. But what exactly does this involve?

The process of progressive discipline includes three stages:

- stage one – giving a verbal warning,
- stage two – giving a written warning, and
- stage three – giving a final written warning.

ELEMENTS OF A VERBAL WARNING

Elements of a verbal warning

The first stage – giving a verbal warning – may be enough to prompt an employee to improve. For the warning you deliver to be effective, you should begin with a statement of the problem. And you should end with a statement of what will happen if there's no improvement.

Statement of the problem

It's important to start a verbal warning by clearly describing the nature of the problem and making it clear why a process of progressive discipline is being followed.

Say an employee continues to arrive late for work every morning after you've already addressed the issue informally. An appropriate opening for a warning is "I'm giving you a formal warning because you've continued to arrive late for work every morning this week, despite our discussion about this."

Statement of what will happen

After explaining the nature of the problem to the employee, end your verbal warning by stating what will happen if the performance problem persists. The employee should be left with no doubt about what will happen if the situation doesn't improve.

For example, end a verbal warning with a statement such as "If you fail to address the problem, you'll receive a written warning, which will be placed in your personnel file and used in your performance appraisal."

It's important to document giving a verbal warning to an employee so there's a record of it. Also ask the employee to sign the written version of the verbal warning. This confirms that the employee received the warning and helps ensure the employee takes the warning seriously.

It's also important to keep the record of a verbal warning in an employee's personnel file, as a record of the first stage in a formal process of progressive discipline.

However, verbal warnings shouldn't affect employees' annual performance grades. Only formal written warnings, delivered in the later stages of the process of progressive discipline, should affect these.

Question

An employee repeatedly fails to submit required performance reports by the deadlines. As his manager, you're now meeting with the employee to give him a verbal warning.

Which two statements are examples of the key elements of an effective verbal warning?

Options:

1. "I'm giving you a formal warning because you've continued to miss deadlines for submitting performance reports."

2. "Not handing your reports in on time means management doesn't have accurate figures when they're needed."

3. "It has come to my attention through my assessment of recent reports that you're still missing deadlines for the submission of your reports."

4. "Continued failure to meet your deadlines will lead to a written warning being placed in your personnel file."

Answer

Option 1: This option is correct. This statement contains one of the key elements of an effective verbal warning and is a good way to start your discussion. It explains why a formal waning is given.

Option 2: This is an incorrect option. Although it helps to know how someone else will be affected if the job isn't done, it doesn't identify the nature of the problem or what steps will be taken if the problem isn't resolved. This statement therefore doesn't contain any of the key elements of an effective verbal warning.

Option 3: This option is incorrect. It's fine for you to mention how you became aware of the problem, but this isn't a key element of a verbal warning.

Option 4: This is a correct option. This statement is a good example of how to end your discussion because it contains a key element of an effective verbal warning. It explains what is going to happen if there's no improvement in the employee's performance.

GUIDELINES FOR GIVING WARNINGS

Guidelines for giving warnings

Any interaction that involves taking disciplinary action against an employee is bound to involve some personal discomfort, for both the manager and the employee.

As a manager, following certain guidelines can help you handle these disciplinary interactions professionally and with the best possible effect. These guidelines apply to all the stages of progressive discipline, whether verbal or written.

The most important guidelines for handling disciplinary interactions can be divided into two main categories – watching your words and involving the employee.

You should generally give employees formal warnings in private. However, sometimes it may be appropriate to include other personnel, such as an employee's supervisor, or a human resources professional.

If you suspect that an employee may become abusive or even violent, you should also consider involving a security officer. You need to watch your words when communicating problem performance. Three guidelines are: never make it personal, don't stifle your employee's motivation, and avoid state-of-mind attributions.

Never make it personal

It's vital to avoid turning a disciplinary interaction into a personal attack. If you do this, you'll just make the employee defensive, and less likely to listen to reason. Instead, focus on the problem. Make it clear that it's the employee's performance, and not the employee's personality, that's your concern.

The kinds of personal statements to avoid might include, "I just don't understand why you're slacking so much," or "You don't seem capable of producing better work." Rather, use less personal statements such as "I'm concerned about the quality of work," or "Certain reports reflect more errors than usual."

Don't stifle motivation

Remain mindful of the impact disciplinary interactions can have on employees. If you don't handle the interactions well, you may crush their enthusiasm and confidence. This is not the way to fix performance problems. Be as specific as possible about the relevant problems and let employees know you're there to assist them. Employees should feel confident that they can improve their performance.

Avoid phrases such as "I don't see how you're going to solve this issue," or "Maybe you're not up to standard." Rather, use statements such as "I can help you address this issue," or "We can turn this around."

Avoid state of mind attributions

As a manager, it's not your job to establish your employees' states of mind. Managers often do this to convey displeasure with bad performance, but all it does is create an extra burden of proof on managers, who have to justify their contentions.

Avoid implying what employees think or feel, or the intentions behind their actions. For example, don't use terms such as insubordinate, consciously, irresponsible, deliberate, or intentionally. You'll have a hard time proving those accusations. Instead of saying "You've been intentionally slacking on this project," say, "We haven't received enough work from you on this project."

Question

What are examples of appropriate statements to use in a disciplinary interaction?

Options:

1. "We can't solve the problem – I just don't think you're capable of learning the required skills."

2. "You've deliberately been taking longer to finish your work."

3. "There's been a steady decline in the quality of your designs."

4. "There's a high rate of errors in your calculations."

Answer

Option 1: This option is incorrect. This statement is unsuitable because it's likely to stifle the employee's motivation, it's personal, and it doesn't offer any assistance.

Option 2: This is an incorrect option. This statement is inappropriate because it sounds like a personal attack and because the word "deliberately" carries an assumption about the employee's state of mind.

Option 3: This is a correct option. This statement is appropriate because it focuses on the problem. It isn't overly personal, isn't likely to stifle the employee's motivation, and doesn't make assumptions about the employee's state of mind.

Option 4: This option is correct. This statement identifies a performance issue without making the conversation personal, stifling the employee's motivation, or using state of mind attributions.

Chavonda manages a team of legal transcriptionists at a top legal firm. She has already approached a team member, Curtis, about his absenteeism, but the problem doesn't seem to have been resolved. Follow along as Chavonda gives Curtis a verbal warning.

Chavonda: Curtis, I called this meeting because I'm concerned about your absenteeism. We dealt with this informally before, but the problem doesn't seem to have been resolved.

Curtis: OK Chavonda. I'm aware of the problem. You see, the thing is, I... Chavonda: Yes, it is a problem and it's one we need to sort out. If there's no improvement soon, I'll have to take more formal disciplinary steps.

Curtis: I understand.

Chavonda: That's good. I expect to notice an immediate improvement. We'll meet again in three weeks to review the situation.

Assessing an interaction

As you may have noted, Chavonda used appropriate language and she stayed focused on the problem. However, she didn't involve Curtis in the interaction as much as she should have and although she expects immediate improvement, she has delayed the follow-up meeting.

It's essential for disciplinary interactions to involve conversations – not just monologues with managers speaking continuously. Employees should be encouraged to participate. Also, though managers should allow adequate time for improvement, it's a good idea to follow up with the employees as soon as possible.

As well as watching what you say, it's important to involve the employee. You should give the employee an opportunity to talk and to ask questions during your interaction. You could, for instance, open the conversation by saying, "As you know, we've discussed your lack of attention to detail before. How do you think you've been doing since that first discussion?" Before ending the discussion, you should also give the employee a chance to have a final say.

Throughout the discussion, let employees comment on what's being discussed if they feel the need and if it's relevant. Also allow time to discuss the issues that have been raised and any other issues that employees consider important.

Then sum up all the key points that have emerged from the meeting and allow employees to comment on and change your summary if necessary.

Although it's important to let employees have their say, you shouldn't go too easy on employees in an attempt to be "fair." Remember that you have to stay in control of the conversation, and remain firm and focused. If you're delivering a verbal warning, the employee has to know there's a problem and understand that you're taking it seriously.

To end any formal warning, it's important to set and communicate the conditions the employee must meet to avoid further disciplinary action. Make sure employees know what they're expected to do and give a time frame for improvement. Point out what would trigger the next stage of progressive discipline.

A formal warning could be ended with a statement of conditions such as "If your customer satisfaction ratings don't improve within the next month, the next step will be a first written warning – which will be recorded in your personnel file."

DELIVERING A VERBAL WARNING

Delivering a verbal warning

So when it comes to giving verbal warnings, remember to state the problem, focus on the problem rather than making it personal, and involve the employee in the discussion. Finally, be sure to communicate the conditions that will trigger the next phase in the disciplinary process.

SECTION 3 - WRITTEN WARNINGS AND FINAL WRITTEN WARNINGS

SECTION 3 - Written Warnings and Final Written Warnings

In the progressive disciplinary process, it is necessary to issue a written warning if an employee fails to meet the conditions of a verbal warning. If the problem persists, a final written warning must be issued. If the final warning is ignored, termination may be the result.

Written warnings must follow the elements of due process and include the current level of warning, an offense description, a written record of prior disciplinary actions, an offense classification, a plan of action the employee can follow to improve, and a clear explanation of the behavior that will trigger the start of the next stage of the disciplinary process.

PRESENTING A WRITTEN WARNING

Presenting a written warning

Say you're locked into a disciplinary process with a consistently underperforming employee. You've given the employee a formal verbal warning – which you've recorded – but transgressions continue. What now? How do you ensure the process results in an outcome favorable to all parties and affords your organization protection? Stage two of the disciplinary process is to present an initial written warning. If this doesn't correct the situation, stage three will see the issuance of a final written warning.

In some instances, an employee's single offense is severe enough to warrant immediate dismissal or a final written warning. A possible example is threatening a colleague. In most cases, though, it's appropriate to give an employee an initial written warning only after a verbal warning has failed to have an effect.

Why give a written warning?

As you may have noted, a written warning indicates that an employee has failed to resolve a performance problem, despite a manager's previous intervention. It may prompt the employee to take the situation more seriously and to make more effort to improve. It may also be used as legal evidence that an organization followed due process in disciplining the employee.

Before you issue a written warning, it may be necessary to put an employee on investigatory suspension – a seldom used measure that gives management time to conduct an independent investigation. Investigatory suspension involves sending the employee home while a potentially serious offense is investigated. When conducting such an investigation, you'll need to gather evidence, interview witnesses, and then present the results to the employee.

Take the example of a team leader who accuses a clerk of using department funds to pay for nonbusiness-related entertainment for a few team members. The initial evidence is compelling, so the clerk is suspended while management gathers more evidence to proceed with the disciplinary process.

Because of the clerk's exemplary record and management's failure to reach agreement on a course of action, the investigating managers decide to place the clerk on investigatory suspension. Management is then able to interview other employees without the possibility of interference or intimidation, determine whether the accusations are justified, and summon the clerk to deliver their findings.

Once any necessary investigation has occurred - and if it's still relevant – you can proceed with giving an employee an initial written warning. You should deliver a written warning in person to underline the seriousness of the matter and to ensure the employee understands what's happening.

PRESENTING A FINAL WRITTEN WARNING

Presenting a final written warning

If a problem persists after you've given an employee an initial written warning, you should move to the third stage – presenting the employee with a final written warning. This means that the conditions set in the first written warning weren't met and the severity of the situation has increased, usually to the point where the employee's job is in danger.

The wording of the warning should make it clear that an employee must comply with specified terms or face a specified consequence – like dismissal. Disciplinary measures that may be instituted before a manager issues a final written warning include suspension without pay, decision-making leave, or probation.

Suspension without pay

Suspension without pay may be used as a form of punishment in cases of deliberate and malicious misconduct to emphasize the severity of an offense. It also removes the relevant employee from the workplace so that this person can't disrupt others.

For example, an administrative assistant whose request for leave has just been turned down intentionally fails to deliver an important phone message to a manager. As a result, the manager misses a meeting and the company loses a potential client. The assistant may be placed on a week's suspension without pay as a form of punishment.

Decision-making leave

Decision-making leave is a short, usually paid, period of leave in which an employee is told to reflect on the relevant performance problem and consider possible solutions. It's appropriate when an employee repeats a transgression without any intention to be malicious, or has demonstrated a serious lack of judgment.

Say a team leader's contract dictates that she must work overtime when required. But even after she receives a warning, she goes home at the usual time and leaves the rest of her team to work longer hours to complete urgent work. Her manager then places her on decision-making leave, suggesting that she take time to think about reaffirming her commitment to the company.

Probation

Putting an employee on probation is similar to issuing a final written warning, except that it involves giving a time limit. Failure to meet specified standards will result in further disciplinary action, like dismissal, once the given time limit is reached.

For example, a sales representative fails to meet minimum monthly sales targets for three months running, despite a final warning. The representative might be put on probation for the next three months. The employee must meet expectations in that time or face dismissal.

Question

Match each disciplinary measure to the example of an employee's behavior that most warrants it. Not all examples will be matched.

Options:

A. Suspension without pay

B. Decision-making leave

Targets:

1. A sales representative intentionally misreports the number of sales she's made in order to qualify for a larger end-of-year bonus

2. An employee leaves important project changes undone and takes a week's leave, without alerting other team members

3. An employee with an otherwise excellent record comes to work up to 30 minutes late every day for a week

Answer

A suspension without pay should be used in cases of wilful and malicious misconduct − like in the case of an employee lying deliberately for personal gain.

Decision-making leave is a short, usually paid, period of leave in which an employee is required to consider an incident of poor performance or bad judgment − like taking leave without alerting team members.

An employee with a good record is unlikely to be at the written warning stage of the progressive disciplinary process. The manager should initiate positive discipline first and then issue a verbal warning before moving on to written warnings.

Although a final written warning is usually the third stage in a process of progressive discipline, it may be appropriate to skip earlier stages. This applies when it would be irresponsible for a manager not to take drastic action immediately – in response to a safety risk, for instance. When determining what stage to start with, you should consider the seriousness of the offense, the employee's performance history, the employee's length of service, and the way you dealt with a similar problem in the past.

COMPONENTS OF WRITTEN WARNINGS

Components of written warnings

At every step of the progressive disciplinary process, it's vital to keep the elements of due process in mind. Employees need to understand expectations and consequences, management needs to implement disciplinary actions consistently, discipline must be appropriate to the offense, and employees must be given opportunities to respond to allegations as well as reasonable periods of time in which to improve.

To ensure due process is followed, a written warning should include certain components, including the current level of warning, a description of the offense, a record of prior disciplinary actions, a classification of the offense, a plan of action the employee can follow to improve, and a clear explanation of what behavior will serve as a trigger for further disciplinary action.

All warnings – even verbal ones – should be documented in full. Written records serve as evidence that due process has been followed. Each record of a warning should identify the current level of warning, provide a detailed description of the subject of the warning, and list any prior disciplinary actions and notifications.

Current level of warning

All warnings – even verbal ones – should be documented in full. Written records serve as evidence that due process has been followed.

For example, "Verbal stage one warning given on January 10, written stage two warning given on May 12, and current warning is stage three final written warning, given on June 4."

Description

The description of the subject should use clear language and detail every aspect of the problem that led to the warning.

For example, "The employee breached the terms of the written warning received on May 12, which triggered this written warning. The employee failed to submit a doctor's note for an unauthorized day of absence, as specified in company guidelines."

Record of prior disciplinary actions

The record of prior disciplinary actions should list all prior warnings the employee has received, even if not clearly linked to the current warning. These should contain descriptions, dates, and actions taken.

For example, "Verbal warning given on January 10 for three instances of absenteeism without doctor's note."

You may have considered the fact that including a written record of all prior notifications about a performance problem can protect an organization legally – for example, if the employee later makes a claim of unfair dismissal.

It provides a record of the steps the organization has taken to alert the employee to a problem and of the opportunities it has given the employee to improve.

It's worth including a record of prior notifications related to other offenses the employee has committed as well. These can help impress the seriousness of the performance problem on the employee and form an overall picture of what constitutes unacceptable behavior.

It's important to classify each offense an employee commits so you can recognize when it's appropriate to progress from giving the employee a verbal warning to taking more serious disciplinary action.

Otherwise you may end up giving an employee a large number of initial warnings for different instances of inappropriate behavior – when actually the behaviors are all examples of the same type of transgression.

You can classify all employee transgressions as one of four main types – policy violations, performance problems, inappropriate conduct, or poor time management and absenteeism. This can help you link superficially separate instances of transgressions so you can handle them through a process of progressive discipline.

Policy violations

Policy violations occur when any company rule is broken. For example, policy violations might include negligent behavior that results in damage to property or loss of profits. The onus is on the employer to show consistency in cases of policy violations – it must be clear that all employees are expected to adhere to the same rules.

Performance problems

Performance problems occur when employees consistently fail to meet work-related expectations.

For example, sales representatives may repeatedly fail to meet minimum sales targets, or programmers may produce only a fraction of the required code during each step of a project.

Inappropriate conduct

Inappropriate conduct refers to any unacceptable employee behavior, including behavior that's illegal, antisocial, disruptive, or in violation of the accepted social or organizational standards. Examples are sexual harassment, insubordination, theft, alcohol abuse, and malicious damage to property.

Poor time management and absenteeism

Poor time management and absenteeism account for a significant number of lost work hours. When such problems persist, they must be dealt with in an appropriately serious manner.

The four types of transgressions overlap. For example, even if an employee commits a range of different transgressions, it may be possible to link them all under general poor conduct or failure to adhere to company policy.

A plan of action should accompany all written warnings and may be included in verbal warnings as well. An action plan lists the concrete steps the errant employee and the employer need to take in order for the problem to be resolved and further discipline avoided.

This plan is related to the elements of due process – a consistent process that makes sure the employee understands the expectations, gives an opportunity to respond and time to improve, and matches appropriate discipline to the offense. This allows the transgressor to respond in each step of the progressive disciplinary process before more serious action comes into effect.

A plan of action in a written warning should typically include four components – improvement goals for the employee, employer responsibilities, employee responsibilities, and supervision and time line details.

Improvement goals

It's important to spell out the tangible performance improvements an employee must make.

Improvement goals set concrete, measurable outcomes for your discipline process.

An example of an improvement goal is "You're expected to begin meeting the specified minimum sales target each month."

Employer responsibilities

The action plan should detail any actions the employer will take – or resources the employer will provide – to help the employee meet the specified improvement goal. This might include providing counseling or training, or even simply providing the employee with a copy of the guidelines or regulations that weren't met. Documenting employer responsibilities indicates what you have done and are doing to help the employee improve.

An example of text describing employer responsibilities in an action plan is "Your supervisor will organize refresher sales training for you on Thursday afternoon, and I have sent you a copy of our sales mission statement to read."

Employee responsibilities

An action plan should detail the employee's responsibilities in terms of meeting the specified improvement goal. In a written action plan, space may be provided for the employee to write a formal response. This satisfies the due process principle of giving an employee the opportunity to respond and participate in the disciplinary process.

In the example action plan, a section on employee responsibilities reads "Each month, you're expected to sell a minimum of 200 units, and the sales must be cleared with the sales manager. If you have questions or wish to discuss these terms, please set up an appointment with me in the next two days."

Supervision and time line

An action plan should specify how long the employee has to demonstrate improvement, how long that necessary level must be maintained, and how this will be monitored. The appropriate time frame and level of supervision will depend on the nature and severity of the offense, and on the stage of the disciplinary process. Allowing a reasonable time frame for improvement is an important part of due process, but this should be specific and include defined dates.

For example, a supervision and time line section could say "You have two months to get your sales figures back up to target. Every two weeks, you'll be required to meet with your sales manager and me to discuss your progress, starting on Friday directly after lunch. After the two month period, you will be expected to maintain an acceptable level of sales."

To uphold due process, it's important that a warning includes a description of the behavior that will trigger the start of the next level of disciplinary action, and what this action will be. For example, the warning may state that the employee with a time management problem must strictly adhere to the company's time management guidelines or face the next disciplinary stage.

This helps ensure the employee is clear about expectations and the consequences of failing to meet these. In such cases, the company would be required to prove that a fair and lawful process took place and that it gave the employee adequate time to address problems.

Question

Match each component of a written warning to a description of why it should be included.

Options:

A. Prior disciplinary actions
B. Classification of offense
C. Employee responsibilities
D. Supervision and time line
E. Conditions for further disciplinary action

Targets:

1. Impresses on the employee the seriousness of actions and documents opportunities given to the employee to improve

2. Allows you to link similar offenses as you progress through the disciplinary process

3. Allows the employee to participate in the disciplinary process and demonstrate concrete improvement

4. Establishes a set period by which performance must have improved and for how long the improvement must be maintained, and how progress will be monitored

5. Clearly sets out what's expected of the employee and what will trigger the next disciplinary stage

Answer

Recording prior disciplinary actions allows you to compare current with previously documented offenses and responses. It may also protect your organization in a legal suit because due process was followed.

Classification of an offense allows you to progress from verbal, to written, and then to final written warnings for offenses that are related – even if they're not identical.

Employee responsibilities give employees a chance to get involved in planning and implementing their own improvement.

Supervision and time line allow you to give an employee a set time in which to improve performance and an indication of how long the employee should maintain that level, and describe the supervision you feel is required.

The conditions for further disciplinary action detail which behavior is expected of the employee and what will cause the next step of the disciplinary process to come into effect.

EXAMPLE OF A FINAL WARNING

Example of a final warning
  Case Study: Question 1 of 3
  Scenario

Take the example of Audrey, a telesales operator for an online insurance broker. She has worked for the company for two years. Over the past few months, Audrey's conduct has deteriorated. She received a verbal warning for repeated rudeness toward customers and a written warning for a repeat of that behavior a month later. Her performance hasn't improved – she recently hung up on a customer who was referred to her. Her manager is now preparing a final written warning.

Answer the questions in order to evaluate the effectiveness of Audrey's final written warning.

  Question

Which additional information should the manager add to the final written warning?

  Options:

1. Details of prior notifications that Audrey received about the problem

2. The goals that Audrey is expected to achieve

3. The responsibilities of both Audrey and her employer

4. Details of how Audrey's performance will be supervised and time lines for doing this

5. A classification of Audrey's offense

Answer

Option 1: This option is correct. A final written warning should detail each prior notification and disciplinary action that the employee received about performance problems. It should specify the stage of the disciplinary process, the date, and a description of each of these actions.

Option 2: This option is correct. A final written warning should clearly state the goals that the employee must achieve to avoid further consequences.

Option 3: This option is incorrect. The final written warning in this case clearly lists the measures the employer will take to ameliorate the problem and the steps Audrey needs to take to keep her job.

Option 4: This is an incorrect option. The final written warning in this example already provides a clear time line and a program for supervision.

Option 5: This option is incorrect. In the warning, the offense is clearly classified as a policy infringement and conduct issue.

Case Study: Question 2 of 3

Which statements accurately critique the final written warning that Audrey's manager drafted?

Options:

1. The disciplinary procedure could be contested because the warning fails to detail opportunities given to Audrey to improve

2. It may mislead Audrey about the seriousness of the offense by not detailing further disciplinary outcomes

3. It leaves the employer open to question by not documenting the assistance the employer is offering to Audrey

4. Audrey could misunderstand what action is required of her

5. It provides a categorization that can link Audrey's recent offenses to similar offenses she may have committed in the past

Answer

Option 1: This option is correct. Due process dictates that the progressive disciplinary process give the employee opportunities to improve before a final written warning is issued. This warning fails to provide a record of those opportunities.

Option 2: This option is incorrect. The warning details further disciplinary outcomes in the results and consequences section.

Option 3: This is an incorrect option. The warning details various actions the employer will take to assist Audrey in improving her performance.

Option 4: This option is correct. The warning does detail specific actions and responsibilities, but it doesn't articulate the general goal that Audrey should be aiming for with respect to her performance.

Option 5: This option is correct. The warning classifies the offense as a policy infringement and conduct issue, which will enable Audrey's manager to connect it to any similar offenses Audrey has committed in the past.

Case Study: Question 3 of 3

Which additional condition could be included in the final written warning?

Options:

1. Decision-making leave
2. Suspension without pay
3. Investigatory suspension
4. Verbal warning

Answer

Option 1: This is an incorrect option. Audrey's conduct issues spill over into inappropriate treatment of customers, so a more punitive measure than decision-making leave may be required.

Option 2: This is the correct option. Suspension without pay is an appropriate disciplinary option for capable employees who demonstrate wilful misconduct.

Option 3: This option is incorrect. Audrey wasn't involved in a dispute with a colleague, her offenses were clearly witnessed, and she had already received a first written warning – usually only delivered after an investigatory suspension. This makes an investigation unnecessary.

Option 4: This is an incorrect option. Audrey's continued offenses have already led to verbal and written warnings, so clearly the first verbal warning was ineffective.

CHAPTER 4 - PREVENTING PROBLEM PERFORMANCE

CHAPTER 4 - Preventing Problem Performance

SECTION 1 - PREVENTING PROBLEMS THROUGH PERFORMANCE MANAGEMENT

SECTION 1 - Preventing Problems Through Performance Management

Effective performance management prevents or minimizes problems in several ways. It motivates employees to perform better, helps managers identify and address problems early – before they become more serious, prevents misunderstandings and errors, and helps identify how an organization can improve.

Elements of performance management that are crucial for preventing problems include planning for performance, monitoring performance, and communicating feedback.

PREVENTING PERFORMANCE PROBLEMS

Preventing performance problems

The success of an organization depends on how well its employees perform. So it's vital not to ignore performance problems or to think of them as the responsibility an individual employee. Instead, managers need to be proactive. They should plan well so they know exactly what level of performance is required, monitor actual performance, and address problems as soon as they emerge. They should also plan in a way that motivates employees to perform well and so avoid problems in the first place.

A performance problem is a discrepancy between the desired performance and the employees' actual performance. So it's the gap between what they should be doing and what they are doing. For example, an employee in a call center is expected to handle 20 calls per hour. This represents the desired performance.

The employee currently handles an average of 10 calls per hour. This is her actual performance. The fact that she actually handles only half the calls she's expected to handle means there's a clear performance problem.

Performance problems are almost always easier to deal with early rather than later. Otherwise the gap between desired and actual performance widens, and problems develop into persistent patterns of poor performance.

If you leave problems until they become serious, you may have to deal with them through drastic disciplinary actions, like dismissal. For an organization, this can be costly and time consuming, and have legal ramifications.

Question

An employee at your company has missed the last two deadlines for submitting reports, although her performance is otherwise good.

How should you handle this situation?

Options:

1. Monitor the employee in case missing deadlines becomes a habit

2. Talk to the employee about the problem over a cup of coffee

3. Give the employee an official warning

Answer

Option 1: This is an incorrect option. A manager should address a problem as early as possible, rather than leaving it to become more serious.

Option 2: This is the correct option. You should act on this problem incident as soon as it emerges and do so informally. Serious employees will appreciate the counsel and change their behavior.

Option 3: This is an incorrect option. It's important to address the problem sooner rather than later. However, you should begin by discussing the problem informally because her behavior is otherwise good. Taking formal disciplinary action is not appropriate in this case.

Detecting performance problems early is important, but it's even better if you can prevent problems completely. It's not possible to prevent every conceivable problem in a workplace full of different people, but managers can take various actions to make performance problems less likely.

Effective performance management begins with a strong culture of performance. In a performance- oriented culture, employees are motivated and have the support they need to perform well.

A performance-oriented culture has specific characteristics:

- employees are thoroughly engaged with their work, so they take responsibility and initiative,
- employees have access to the support and resources they need,
- employees work well as team members, without backbiting or negative rivalry,
- employees collaborate in a community of support and learning, for example using wikis and forums,
- employees know how their tasks relate to the overall goals of the organization,
- employees plan their own improvement and development, and
- managers support the program of performance management.

Performance management involves an ongoing, collaborative process of communication between a manager and an employee. It's about talking, listening, learning, and improving.

Its goal is to encourage employees continually to assess their performance and to map out and follow steps for improving.

PERFORMANCE MANAGEMENT

Performance management

When you manage performance effectively, you need to perform certain activities. You need to be prepared to clarify job functions and standards, explain how an employee's contributions help achieve a company's organizational goals, resolve performance problems together with the employee whose performance is not satisfactory, establish how to measure performance, and identify and then remove obstacles to good performance.

Clarify functions and standards

It's important to clarify employees' job functions and associated standards so that both you and they know exactly what performance is expected.

For example, a copy editor in a publishing house is expected to edit a certain number of words of copy per day. This requirement should be clearly defined and explained at the start of the copy editor's employment, and whenever this expectation changes.

Explain contributions

If employees know how their daily tasks contribute to the "bigger picture" of an organization's business goals, they're more likely to understand what performance is required.

For example, administrative clerks working in a bank should know that when they process customer transactions correctly and speedily, they help the bank fulfill one of its goals, which is to provide fast and efficient service.

Resolve problems together

It's important that you and the employee work together at resolving the problem. This lets the employee know that there's a system in place and that you'll be providing support.

Measure performance

You and the employee should agree on exactly how the employee's performance will be measured. For example, a call center agent who fails to meet her daily customer calls needs to know how many calls she needs to make in a day and how many calls need to result in a sale. You may want to provide her with a spreadsheet in which she can record her numbers.

Identify and remove obstacles

On an ongoing basis, you and an employee should collaborate in identifying and removing obstacles to good performance. Examples of these obstacles could be poor time management or a lack of required skills.

The concept of performance management isn't always well understood. Common misconceptions are that it involves one-way intervention, is used to address problem situations only, is essentially the same as a performance appraisal, and largely involves criticism or prodding of employees.

One-way intervention

Performance management is not meant to be a one-way intervention during which managers force performance standards on employees. It should be a collaborative process.

Problem situations only

You should use performance management to address problem situations, but you can also use it to provide continuous feedback to those who are performing according to standard, in an effort to find better ways of doing the same job. It can therefore be implemented on an ongoing basis.

Same as performance appraisal

Performance management includes holding performance appraisals, but it also involves planning jobs, diagnosing problems, identifying obstacles to good performance, and developing employees' skills and knowledge.

Criticism or prodding

Performance management shouldn't involve criticizing or prodding – or urging – employees to improve their performance. Instead, it should be a collaborative growing process, designed to facilitate good performance.

Strong performance management helps prevent problems because it takes a proactive rather than reactive approach. It involves anticipating what needs to be done and how to develop and improve capabilities. For example, an employee in a design agency might work with her manager to determine how best to improve her efficiency, in line with a drive to boost the agency's output.

Sorin Dumitrascu

Performance management involves regular communication about performance and organizational goals, which helps motivate employees to perform well.

For example, employees who debug software in a software development company are much more likely to be motivated if they're regularly given information about the projects and clients their company are considering and about how their individual efforts are contributing to its success.

The monitoring that forms part of performance management helps ensure that managers detect problems early, before they become serious. For example, if you discover that an employee is struggling to use an accounting package correctly, you and the employee can address the problem before it causes serious delays or results in errors that are passed on to the customer.

Finally, performance management often sheds light on where and how an organization can improve to assist employees in being more effective and efficient. For example, it may be necessary to provide employees with a more intuitive accounting system or to train them to use new accounting software.

Question

Which statements about performance management are true?

Options:

1. It's essentially the same as performance appraisals
2. It's a collaborative process
3. It's relevant only when staff are performing poorly
4. It relies on managers telling employees what to do
5. It involves anticipating and removing potential obstacles to good performance

6. It largely involves criticizing poor performance and pushing employees to do better

Answer

Option 1: This is an incorrect option. Performance management goes beyond just appraising performance. It involves managers and employees planning, diagnosing problems, finding solutions, and developing skills to optimize performance.

Option 2: This is a correct option. Effective performance management depends on close collaboration between managers and their employees.

Option 3: This is an incorrect option. Performance management should involve planning, monitoring, and optimizing the performance of all employees – not just of poor performers.

Option 4: This is an incorrect option. Effective performance management is collaborative. Managers and employees work together to plan, monitor, and improve performance.

Option 5: This option is correct. Effective performance management is proactive. It involves planning ahead, and anticipating needed performance as well as potential obstacles to this.

Option 6: This is an incorrect option. Effective performance management is about managers and employees working together to improve performance – rather than about managers criticizing employees or simply telling them what to do.

Preventing problems through performance management involves three main elements:

- planning for performance,
- monitoring performance, and

• communicating feedback.

These three elements are part of a cyclical process. When you plan for performance, you determine the requirements an employee needs to meet. You monitor performance because you want to ensure that actual performance meets the desired requirements you planned for. And you communicate feedback so that everyone is aware of the progress in performance. This information then feeds into your performance planning activities, and so the cycle continues.

Question

How does effective performance management help prevent or minimize performance problems?

Options:

1. It motivates employees to perform well
2. It ensures employees know that poor performance will have severe consequences
3. It makes it easier for employers to dismiss poor performers
4. It helps highlight areas where an organization can improve
5. It helps managers identify problems early
6. It helps prevent misunderstandings and errors

Answer

Option 1: This is a correct option. Performance management motivates employees through regular communication about their performance and about how their efforts support larger organizational goals.

Option 2: This is an incorrect option. Performance management doesn't involve threatening employees. It relies on managers and employees working as partners to optimize performance.

Option 3: This option is incorrect. The goal of performance management isn't to provide employers with pretexts for dismissing poor performers. Its goal is to assist employees in improving their performance.

Option 4: This is a correct option. Planning and receiving ongoing feedback from employees help managers identify how to improve the support an organization provides for good performance.

Option 5: This option is correct. Ongoing monitoring helps ensure that managers detect performance problems early, before they become more serious.

Option 6: This is a correct option. Performance management helps prevent misunderstandings and errors because it involves regular communication between managers and employees.

SECTION 2 - PLANNING FOR PERFORMANCE

SECTION 2 - Planning for Performance

During the performance planning process, it's imperative that you communicate expectations related to work priorities and the responsibilities of both the employee and the employer. You should do this in a way that's collaborative, involving the employee and asking open-ended questions.

It's also important to use the planning stage to motivate employees. To do this, you should set specific performance objectives, explain how employees' tasks align with organizational goals, and explain how meeting expectations will personally benefit the employees.

THE PLANNING STAGE

The planning stage

Performance planning is the first step in preventing performance problems. Having employees participate in this planning helps ensure they understand how their tasks link to organizational goals, what performance expectations they should meet, how success will be measured, and what support managers will provide.

The planning process should result in a document that can be referenced throughout the year. Planning may take place when an employee is first employed, but should also be revisited at least annually thereafter. Most often, plans are updated or altered during performance review meetings.

The process of planning performance has two main purposes – to communicate expectations and to motivate employees.

COMMUNICATING EXPECTATIONS

Communicating expectations

The expectations you should communicate to employees during the planning stage include those related to work priorities, employee responsibilities, and employer responsibilities.

Work priorities

The challenge of competing work priorities is a reality most employees face. When every task seems important, it can be difficult to allocate time appropriately. Employees need to understand which aspects of their work take priority over others and under what conditions, so they don't spend too much time on less important tasks.

Employee responsibilities

Employees should have a good understanding of their responsibilities, how they contribute to organizational goals, and what kind of performance is expected of them. They should know what tasks they're expected to complete, and how much flexibility there is in their job descriptions.

Employer responsibilities

Employers are responsible for providing employees with the support and resources they need to do their jobs – and employees should know what types of support they can count on getting.

Employers should play a role in promoting continuous learning and the sharing of knowledge. They should also remove obstacles as needed and coordinate employees' efforts.

It's important to document the expectations you communicate so that both you and the employee can access these again whenever necessary.

However, it's not enough just to hand over a written list of expectations. For this process to contribute to better performance, you need to communicate expectations collaboratively. You should involve the employee, drawing on this person's insights and ensuring you agree about what's required.

To communicate collaboratively with employees, you should ask open-ended questions that elicit their opinion and input. Open-ended questions are questions that encourage full responses with information, opinions, and input. Closed-ended questions are questions that require only a "yes," "no," or single-word response.

To communicate collaboratively, you can ask open-ended questions about the employee's job description, about how the employee's work links to organizational goals, and about what obstacles there are to fulfilling the expectations of the job. You can also ask what the employee thinks about the effectiveness of management support, the measurement of progress and success, and work goals.

Job description

You can ask questions like "How accurate do you feel your job description is?" and "How do you think it can be improved?"

An employee may have valuable suggestions for more accurately outlining the responsibilities of the job – and you can then update the job description.

Organizational goals

You can get an idea of how well employees understand how their work contributes to organizational goals by asking questions such as "How do you think your work helps achieve our organizational goals?" and "How do you prioritize your work tasks according to organizational goals?"

It can help motivate employees if they have an in-depth understanding of their work's value to the company or of how it ties in with organizational goals.

Obstacles

To discuss the obstacles of a job, you can ask questions such as "Do you come across any obstacles when you are trying to complete your work?" and "If so, what are they and how can they be resolved or avoided?"

This will help you become aware of any issues that you can help an employee overcome.

Support

You can show employees they have management support by asking questions such as "Do you feel management could do more to help you complete your work tasks?" and "If so, what can they do to help?"

These will help you determine where you can provide assistance for an employee.

Measurement

You can involve employees in their progress by asking questions such as "What do you feel is the best way to measure your progress and success? What are your reasons?"

Employees can give you insight into the best ways of appraising their performance. This can also be the starting point for a motivating discussion about career development goals.

Feasible goals

An employee is qualified for a particular job and generally knows what the job entails. As a result, it's a good idea to ask what the employee believes is realistically achievable.

Examples of questions you can ask are "What do you feel are feasible goals to set for yourself on a monthly basis?" and "How often do you think progress reviews should take place?"

Bruce, a manager in a recruitment company, has just hired a new researcher, Carrie, and needs to explain what is expected of her with regards to performance. Follow along as Bruce explains the expectations to Carrie in a performance planning meeting.

Bruce: In our company, we like to measure employees' performance regularly to help them achieve their goals.

Carrie: That sounds like a very good idea.

Bruce: You've done a similar job previously. What do you feel is the best way to measure your progress?

Carrie: Well, I think it would be good to consider the number of clients I handle over a period of time.

Bruce: Here we generally measure your progress by the number of successful placements that you achieve.

Carrie: Oh, OK.

Bruce: How can I help and assist you as you get started in your new role?

Carrie: I expect some initial startup problems in identifying the people of interest to our company. Could you perhaps provide me access to the client database?

Bruce: Yes, that's a good idea.

Bruce: I think we'll set you a goal of achieving two successful placements per month - does that sound OK to you?

Carrie: OK, that sounds good.

Question

Which of Bruce's statements are appropriate examples of collaborative communication?

Options:

1. "You've done a similar job previously – what do you feel is the best way to measure your progress?"

2. "Here we generally measure your progress by the number of successful placements that you achieve."

3. "How can I help and assist you as you get started in your new role?"

4. "I think we'll set you a goal of achieving two successful placements per month - does that sound OK to you?"

Answer

Option 1: This option is correct. Bruce involves Carrie in her performance planning by asking her how best to measure her progress.

Option 2: This is an incorrect option. Although Bruce asks for Carrie's opinion during their discussion, he doesn't take it into account. Instead, he imposes his own idea without suggesting that he's first considered hers.

Option 3: This is a correct option. Bruce collaborates with Carrie, and makes it clear that he'll support her, by asking how he can assist her as she gets started in her new role.

Option 4: This option is incorrect. Bruce fails to ask Carrie an open-ended question to give her a chance to voice her opinion and requirements. Instead, he asks a closed-ended question, which leads to a short response.

MOTIVATING EMPLOYEES

Motivating employees

It's important to motivate employees to perform at their best throughout all the stages of performance management. During the planning stage, you should therefore set specific objectives to focus employee effort, align employee objectives with larger organizational goals, and explain the benefits of meeting the expectations you've communicated.

Set specific objectives

Giving an employee specific objectives to work toward achieving can help focus the employee's efforts, clarify what needs to be done, and motivate good performance.

For example, an employee who is simply told to increase productivity isn't likely to feel as driven to achieve as much as an employee who is asked to increase the number of completed projects by 25%. Specific targets give people concrete results to aim for.

Align with organizational goals

You can help motivate employees by making it clear how their work makes a difference in the organization –

or how it contributes to broader organizational goals. To do this, you need to be familiar with the organization's short- and long-term goals and strategies, as well as with the employee's responsibilities.

For example, a customer-service employee who understands that providing clients with excellent service builds client loyalty and trust, therefore increasing overall business and success, is more likely to produce higher quality work. And when satisfied customers provide positive feedback to the company, it will reinforce this connection between the employee's work and the organization's success.

Explain the benefits

One of the best ways to motivate employees is to explain how it will benefit them personally if they meet the specified performance expectations. For example, continued good performance may lead to promotions, pay raises, and career advancement.

You should also explain how the performance management process itself can benefit employees. For example, it can give employees a better understanding of work priorities and ensure they know what to expect.

Frank has just been hired to lead a team that manufactures a line of furniture for a furniture design company. His manager, Dominique, meets with him to discuss performance expectations and plans. Follow along as Dominique explains expectations to Frank.

Dominique: Hi, Frank. Thanks for taking the time to meet with me. As you know, we'll be measuring your progress over time in your new position. Your job is to make your team work better.

173

Frank: Can we discuss what's involved in that expectation?

Dominique: Your main goal is to increase the productivity of your team. One of the company's key strategic goals is to increase the profitability of this line of products.

Frank: Right, so my main objective is to boost production – and this will help the company overall?

Dominique: Yes exactly. Achieving higher team productivity will be good for you too.

Frank: Oh?

Dominique: Yes. The percentage of the productivity increase every six monthswill go toward the calculation of a bonus for you.

Frank: OK, great.

Dominique: I think you're really going to enjoy working with this team.

Question

Which of Dominique's statements are likely to help motivate Frank?

Options:

1. "Your main goal is to increase the productivity of your team."

2. "The percentage of the productivity increase every six months will go toward the calculation of a bonus for you."

3. "Your job is to make your team work better."

4. "I think you're really going to enjoy working with this team."

5. "One of the company's key strategic goals is to increase the profitability of this line of products."

Answer

Option 1: This option is correct. Setting a specific objective – like increasing productivity – is a good way to motivate an employee.

Option 2: This is a correct option. Dominique explains how meeting expectations will benefit Frank by telling him about a bonus that will be tied to any increases in the productivity of his team.

Option 3: This option is incorrect. Dominique's statement about making his team work better is too vague. It doesn't clarify what's expected, nor does it motivate Frank by giving him a clear objective.

Option 4: This is an incorrect option. This statement doesn't explain why Dominique thinks Frank will enjoy working with the team. To motivate employees, you need to explain to them how they will benefit.

Option 5: This is a correct option. You can help motivate employees by explaining how their work will contribute to the overall organizational goals. Dominique explains to Frank that his main goal of increasing productivity will help increase the company's strategic goal of increasing profitability.

SECTION 3 - MONITORING PERFORMANCE

SECTION 3 - Monitoring Performance

It's important to use objective evidence when making major decisions related to problem performances. You can obtain such evidence by monitoring employee performance. Monitoring techniques include observation, 360-degree feedback, bi-directional evaluation, and self-assessment and self-reporting.

Guidelines for using these techniques include ensuring your methods are unobtrusive, involving the employee in the process, using representative sampling, and documenting the data you obtain.

PERFORMANCE MONITORING BEST PRACTICES

Performance monitoring best practices

Decisions about disciplinary actions and termination of employment can have far-reaching effects for your organization and its people. So you can't rely on instinct alone when making these decisions. You must base the decisions on solid evidence.

To acquire such evidence, you have to monitor employees' performance. This involves periodically collecting and checking data about their performance.

Monitoring can help prevent problems. It enables you to detect and address performance issues before they become persistent or serious. Records of the data you collect can also help you justify important performance-related decisions.

To support performance monitoring, you gather and organize relevant performance-related data about employees. This data can come from a variety of sources – both quantitative and qualitative.

Quantitative

Quantitative performance data relates to the quantity, or volume, of work employees do. Examples are statistics about how quickly customers are served, or how many units of a product a salesperson sells. These measures reveal employees' efficiency and productivity.

Qualitative

Qualitative data about performance relates to the quality of employees' work. You can source this type of data from comments in customer feedback forms and from results of quality tests and reviews.

If you use unreliable or faulty data to assess employees' performance, your employment-related decisions will be faulty too. So it's important to use a sound process for gathering performance-related data.

For performance monitoring to be effective, follow four main guidelines: be unobtrusive, involve the employee, use representative sampling, and document the data.

It's important to avoid making data collection a burden that disrupts the work of employees. Try not to disturb their work or to assign additional data-collection tasks that will interfere with their core work. And avoid collecting unnecessary data. Limit your data collection to that which will help you prevent problems.

Say a manager wants to monitor how employees are spending their time. The system for gathering this data could either be obtrusive or unobtrusive.

Obtrusive

A manager forces employees to fill out an hourly time sheet, along with details about each completed task. The employees resent this level of monitoring because they now don't have the time to complete their actual work efficiently. They start to resent the time sheet system, which results in careless mistakes when filling them out.

Unobtrusive

A manager asks employees to fill out a weekly time sheet which contains a space for recording comments about difficulties they encountered. The employees appreciate this level of monitoring as it doesn't take much time. It also leads to productive discussions that help employees and managers resolve obstacles that would otherwise not have been reported.

It's important to at least to tell employees why and how often you'll be monitoring their performance. But if you involve them more in the process by eliciting their input, they'll be more likely to support and accept the monitoring.

For example, let employees suggest what type of monitoring to implement and how often this monitoring should occur.

Or get employees to help you collect data, for example by giving you status reports for ongoing projects. Of course, you'll need to choose a relatively unobtrusive data-collection approach.

Another important guideline is to use representative sampling. It's usually not feasible to monitor every aspect of an employee's performance all the time. But the sample data you gather must accurately represent the employee's overall performance, if this is what you're going to draw conclusions about.

For instance, it wouldn't be appropriate to base general conclusions about an employee's performance only on this person's output during the first hour of each day. Instead,

179

you should record the employee's output at a range of different times and under different circumstances.

Question

A courier company's supervisor wants to determine how satisfied customers are with an employee's service over the course of a month. To do this, he reviews the customer feedback forms which are filled out for each of the employee's 100 deliveries that month.

Which option is a representative sample?

Options:

1. 100 forms throughout the entire month
2. 20 forms at different times of the month
3. 15 deliveries at month-end

Answer

Option 1: This option is incorrect. A representative sample does not take all 100 instances in the month. It only takes a sample of these 100.

Option 2: This is the correct option. A representative sample takes instances from different times of the month.

Option 3: This is an incorrect option. A representative sample takes instances from different times of the month – not just at the end of the month, for example.

A final guideline is to document the performance-related data you gather. This is important because it gives you a physical record of information which you can review when you need to make decisions. You can also use it to support your arguments when you need to explain your reasons for a particular decision to an employee.

You can include several types of information when documenting performance:

- achievement of set goals or standards,

- evidence of the quality of employees' work,
- praise, criticism, or complaints about employees or their work, and
- information revealing the causes of problems or successes.

Achievement

The customer sales rep meets her submission target of 20 signed-up customers for the month. The programmer only submits 95% of code lines he's expected to submit by the end of the month.

Quality of work

The customer sales rep's records about her customers are without fault. She also follows up on all customer queries she can't resolve immediately within the stipulated 24 hours.

The programmer doesn't test his code lines, which results in a software malfunction hours before it's due to be presented to the client.

Praise, criticism, or complaints

The customer sales rep receives excellent service reviews from her customers.

Other programmers complain about the number of times they have to help the programmer fix code or teach him standard coding practices.

Causes of problems or successes

The customer sales rep's monthly time sheet reveals she sometimes works after hours to complete her admin work and research queries she wasn't able to resolve during the day.

The programmer's weekly feedback report reveals that his computer malfunctioned almost every day and he was unable to produce high-quality code due to these malfunctions.

Generally, such documentation isn't stored in employees' personnel files. The documents are for managers' own records. However, some documents may be included as summary information in employees' regular performance appraisals.

Question

Which actions are in keeping with the guidelines for effective monitoring of employee performance?

Options:

1. Calculating average customer satisfaction based on ratings in ten end-of-month customer survey forms

2. Asking employees for advice on effective ways to monitor time wastage at work

3. Asking team members to document cases where colleagues who failed to submit preceding reports on time caused delays

4. Ensuring you don't distract employees when observing how well they handle a process

5. Assessing the accuracy of a sales clerk's transactions at several different times over the course of a week

6. Requiring employees to compile a daily list of every work task they perform

Answer

Option 1: This is an incorrect option. This style of monitoring takes one specific instance of data into account, instead of a representative sample of the data in different instances.

Option 2: This option is correct. Involving employees can improve the results of monitoring and earn their support for it.

Option 3: This is a correct option. This style of monitoring documents causes of problems, such as delays caused by colleagues.

Option 4: This option is correct. This style of monitoring is unobtrusive because it doesn't disturb employees from their work.

Option 5: This is a correct option. It's important to ensure representative sampling – for example by recording performance at different times and under different circumstances.

Option 6: This option is incorrect. This style of monitoring is obtrusive because it gives employees more work and may have a negative impact on their performance.

OBSERVATION

Observation

You can monitor employee performance using several techniques, including observation, 360-degree feedback, bi-directional evaluation, and self-assessment and self-reporting. To get a complete picture of employee performance, you should try to apply as many of the techniques as you can. However, because each involves time and costs, it may not be feasible to use all of them.

The frequency of monitoring you perform and the area you monitor should depend on factors like an employee's experience level and role, familiarity with tasks, the type of work the employee does, and the organization's goals.

Experience level

New employees, or those in junior positions, require more frequent monitoring than those who've been in their jobs for several years.

Familiarity with tasks

Employees performing tasks that are fairly new to them should be monitored more frequently than those performing more familiar tasks.

Type of work

The type of work an employee does will help determine which areas of performance should be monitored most often. For example, interaction with customers will be a predominant area of monitoring for salespeople, whereas quality or quantity might be most important for employees on a production line.

Goals

The time frames for achieving organizational goals should affect the frequency of monitoring. For example, if you aim to increase product sales over the course of a year, monthly monitoring may be suitable. But if you need to increase daily production rates, monitoring should happen daily.

Question

An online business consultancy employs Javier – an experienced copywriter who also occasionally does graphic design work for the company's web site. The company wants to double its web traffic over the next few months, and recognizes Javier's articles as a means to help achieve this goal.

Which is the most appropriate monitoring plan in this case?

Options:

1. Check up on Javier's work rate twice a day

2. Track the quality of Javier's graphic design projects daily

3. Monitor the number of new articles Javier publishes each week

Answer

Option 1: This is an incorrect option. Although Javier's role is important, his experience means he shouldn't be monitored so frequently.

Option 2: This option is incorrect. Graphic design isn't Javier's main job and it isn't important in terms of the company's goal. So it's not appropriate to monitor this aspect of his work on a daily basis.

Option 3: This is the correct option. It's relevant to monitor the number of articles that Javier publishes because they relate directly to the company's goal. Also, it's appropriate to monitor them only once a week because Javier is an experienced copywriter.

Observation involves watching employees as a means of monitoring their performance. It's especially useful because it gives you solid evidence, in the form of what you personally see or hear about an employee's behavior.

For example, if you notice an employee working after hours one evening in order to meet a deadline, you've observed dedication from that employee. Observation isn't based on what you hear from others. For example, if an employee tells you that his colleague arrives late to work every day, it's not observation, because you didn't see this happening.

One common observation technique is "management by walking around." This simply involves walking around the workplace, observing what's going on and engaging with employees about their work. In this way, you can keep in touch with employees' concerns and collect data about how work is proceeding.

Aside from management by walking around, you can make observations from several other reliable sources of information:

- reviews of completed work,
- customer feedback data,
- quality or quantity metrics, and
- other results or measures of work.

The purposes of observation are performance detection and performance analysis.

Performance detection

By observing employees, you can detect good or poor performance.

For example, you might observe a sales representative's interaction with customers to determine whether the representative is meeting required standards for customer service.

Performance analysis

You can analyze the performance of employees to help determine the reasons for good or poor performance.

Say a bank employee processes transactions 30% faster than her colleagues. You may observe her while she's working to identify what she does that makes her especially efficient. You can then share her methods with other employees.

Question

Match each purpose of observation with examples of data-gathering that serve this purpose. A purpose may match to more than one example.

Options:

A. Performance detection

B. Performance analysis

Targets:

1. Monitor how long the office administrator takes to answer the phone

2. Keep track of the number of customer complaints received per week

3. Identify which employees are most often the target of customer complaints

4. Examine the background of cases where employees verbally abused their colleagues

Answer

Monitoring call answering metrics helps you detect whether the administrator is meeting the required expectations.

Following customer feedback helps you detect whether your employees are mistreating customers.

Identifying which employees receive the most complaints helps you analyze the reasons and patterns surrounding the mistreatment of customers.

Examining the history behind instances of verbal abuse helps you analyze the reasons behind these incidents.

360-DEGREE FEEDBACK

360-degree feedback

360-degree feedback is performance-related feedback from a range of people who interact with an employee. It can create a more complete picture of an employee's performance than feedback from any one source.

Your answer might have included several sources of 360-degree feedback, such as your manager, colleagues, internal customers, clients, and even suppliers. Because the feedback incorporates different perspectives, it's useful for both problem management and employee evaluations.

Problem management

Collecting 360-degree feedback increases your ability to identify problems because it shows how the employee's work and behavior affects customers, colleagues, and even suppliers.

Employee evaluations

By incorporating information from numerous sources, 360-degree feedback makes employee evaluations more objective. This can help ensure employees accept the evaluations.

To collect 360-degree feedback, you first need to develop feedback forms. You can develop these forms yourself or with the assistance of employees, customers, and suppliers. And the forms can be paper- based or electronic.

Typically, these forms ask respondents to rate the employee's performance on a predefined scale, such as 1 to 10, in various areas such as handling of job responsibilities, ability to meet deadlines, and commitment to company goals.

You should distribute the form to all those who work with the employee on a regular basis. This could include the employee's colleagues, team leader, and subordinates, as well as internal customers, clients, and suppliers.

These people should submit their responses anonymously so they feel free to give honest answers. After collecting the results, you summarize the ratings – either manually or using specialized software. Although 360-degree feedback is useful, it also has disadvantages. Because so much information is involved, it can be expensive, time consuming, and complex to compile.

Additionally, because 360-degree feedback typically uses rating scales, the information collected isn't as precise as it could be. This also means that the information may not be objective enough to protect companies that take disciplinary action.

BI-DIRECTIONAL EVALUATION

Bi-directional evaluation

As the name implies, bi-directional evaluation means that feedback flows in two directions – from manager to employee, and from employee to manager. This type of evaluation is beneficial because it gives managers feedback on how well they're meeting the needs of their employees.

The feedback can either be formal or informal. To initiate informal feedback, you just need to ask employees how you can help them do their jobs better. For bi-directional evaluation to be effective, both sides – the manager and the employees – need to have several qualities.

Manager

The manager needs to trust the employees and not suspect that they will give dishonest feedback. The manager also needs to have good interpersonal skills, and must be able to receive negative feedback in a calm, professional, and nondefensive manner.

Employees

Employees need to trust the manager and be confident that any criticism leveled at the manager will be accepted without retribution or negative impact on them. Employees also need to be honest in their feedback, and avoid statements that are politically motivated or insulting to the manager.

SELF-ASSESSMENT AND SELF-REPORTING

Self-assessment and self-reporting

Asking employees to assess or report on their own performance can encourage them to buy in to the process. It can make them open to identifying problems in their performance and to taking steps to improve.

Regularly asking employees about their work – whether in writing or formal conversations – can give you a starting point for performance-related discussions. Getting employees' perspectives can also help you anticipate differences of opinion that may arise during performance assessments.

You can choose to provide employees with a self-assessment form, asking that they rate various aspects of their performance. For example, a form could have employees rate their performance of different tasks on a scale of 1 to 10. It could also include a space for comments.

Managers may worry that employees will give themselves higher performance ratings than they actually deserve.

Although this is a risk, the reality is that most employees are more critical of their performance than their managers are likely to be.

Question

Match the monitoring techniques to the statements that describe them. A technique may match to more than one example.

Options:

A. 360-degree feedback

B. Bi-directional evaluation

C. Self-assessment or self-reporting

Targets:

1. Assists in problem management by including information from multiple sources

2. Involves two-way feedback between an employee and a manager

3. Involves employees in the monitoring process, which helps managers anticipate differences in opinion

4. Involves collecting performance ratings, usually anonymously

5. Can be informal, but requires good interpersonal skills on the part of a manager

Answer

360-degree feedback increases your ability to identify problem areas by collecting ratings-based information from multiple people that an employee interacts with, such as colleagues and supervisors.

Bi-directional evaluation involves two-way feedback between an employee and a manager – about the employee's performance, and about the manager's performance in terms of meeting the employee's needs.

Self-assessment engages employees, giving managers an idea of different perceptions that exist about employee performance.

360-degree feedback is usually provided anonymously, in the form of performance ratings in various categories.

In bi-directional evaluation, the manager needs to be able to handle negative feedback calmly and professionally.

Case Study: Question 1 of 3
Scenario

Stefan, who works for an event management company, is leading a project that involves planning a convention. Tamara has been monitoring his performance.

Access the learning aid Monitoring Stefan's Performance to help you answer the questions. Practice your knowledge of performance monitoring by answering the questions in order.

Question

What does Tamara achieve with her approach to monitoring Stefan's work?

Options:

1. Monitoring the progress of the project schedule helps her understand why Stefan excels in some areas

2. Reviewing documents helps her gauge the level of quality of Stefan's written work

3. Talking about Stefan's shortcomings helps her better understand Stefan's areas of weakness

4. Getting survey feedback from team members helps her understand why Stefan struggles with some tasks

Answer

Option 1: This is an incorrect option. Tracking project progress via the schedule tells Tamara how well Stefan is doing, but doesn't help her understand the reasons for his performance.

Option 2: This option is correct. By checking Stefan's completed work, Tamara can detect how well he performs in terms of meeting the company's quality standards.

Option 3: This is a correct option. By discussing Stefan's poor performance, Tamara can analyze the reasons behind it.

Option 4: This option is incorrect. The surveys are ratings-based, which means that they can only help Tamara detect problems. They don't give her insight about the reasons for the problems.

Case Study: Question 2 of 3

Which statements accurately describe the monitoring approach Tamara is using?

Options:

1. The monitoring gives Stefan the opportunity for self-evaluation

2. The monitoring includes an aspect where Stefan comments on Tamara's performance

3. The monitoring seeks the perspectives of those who work with Stefan

4. The monitoring requires Stefan and Tamara to have great trust in each other

Answer

Option 1: This is a correct option. Tamara uses the technique of employee self-assessment by asking Stefan to evaluate his own performance via a monthly survey.

Option 2: This is an incorrect option. Tamara doesn't use bi-directional evaluation, which would involve having

Stefan appraise her performance as well as giving him feedback about his performance.

Option 3: This option is correct. Tamara uses 360-degree feedback via a survey that seeks the perspectives of Stefan's team members every two weeks.

Option 4: This option is incorrect. Tamara isn't using bi-directional evaluation, which requires a trusting manager-employee relationship.

Case Study: Question 3 of 3

Which recommendations are best practices Tamara uses as she monitors Stefan's performance?

Options:

1. She uses Stefan's submitted documents as part of her monitoring

2. She monitors Stefan's work infrequently

3. She surveys a broad array of people who interact with Stefan and his work

4. She allows Stefan to set the frequency of self-assessment

Answer

Option 1: This option is correct. By including documented information in monitoring – in this case, submitted documents – Tamara ensures that her monitoring makes use of reliable data.

Option 2: This is an incorrect option. Tamara monitors Stefan's performance every week, which is justified because of Stefan's inexperience and the importance of the project.

Option 3: This option is incorrect. Tamara's survey is limited to only the members of Stefan's team.

Option 4: This is a correct option. By asking Stefan to assess his own performance and asking how often he'd like to complete the self-assessment survey, Tamara involves him in the process.

REFERENCES

References
1. **How to Be an Even Better Manager: A Complete A–Z of Proven Techniques & Essential Skills, Seventh Edition** - 2008, Michael Armstrong, Kogan Page
2. **Analyzing Performance Problems: or You Really Oughta Wanna, Third Edition** - 1997, Robert F. Mager and Peter Pipe, CEP Press
3. **Beyond Training and Development: The Groundbreaking Classic on Human Performance Enhancement, Second Edition** - 2005, William J. Rothwell, AMACOM
4. **Performance Management** - 1999, Robert Bacal, McGraw-Hill
5. **Perfect Phrases for Documenting Employee Performance Problems** - 2005, Anne Bruce, McGraw-Hill
6. **The Human Element: Understanding and Managing Employee Behavior** - 2007, Lee Roy Beach, M. E. Sharpe, Inc.

7. **Improving Employee Performance through Workplace Coaching: A Practical Guide to Performance Management** - 2005, Earl M.A. Carter and Frank A. McMahon, Kogan Page

8. **The Evaluation Interview: How to Probe Deeply, Get Candid Answers, and Predict the Performance of Job Candidates, Fifth Edition** - 2002, Richard Fear and Robert Chiron, McGraw-Hill

9. **The Communication Problem Solver: Simple Tools and Techniques for Busy Managers** - 2010, Nannette Rundle Carroll

10. **101 Sample Write-Ups for Documenting Employee Performance Problems: A Guide to Progressive Discipline and Termination, Second Edition** - 2010, Paul Falcone, AMACOM

11. **The First-Time Manager, Fifth Edition** - 2005, Loren B. Belker and Gary S. Topchik, AMACOM

12. **101 Tough Conversations to Have with Employees: A Manager's Guide to Addressing Performance, Conduct, and Discipline Challenges** - 2009, Paul Falcone, AMACOM

13. **Performance Management** - 1999, Robert Bacal, McGraw-Hill

14. **Action Tools for Effective Managers: A Guide for Solving Day-to-Day Problems on**

the Job - 2000, Margaret Mary Gootnick and David Gootnick, AMACOM
15. **Analyzing Performance Problems: or You Really Oughta Wanna, Third Edition** - 1997, Robert F. Mager and Peter Pipe, CEP Press
16. **The Management Bible** - 2005, Bob Nelson and Peter Economy, John Wiley & Sons
17.

GLOSSARY

Glossary

A

ability - Capacity, acquired or innate.

B

benchmark - An industry best or level of achievement against which performance can be measured.

bi-directional evaluation - A monitoring technique in which feedback about performance flows in two directions; from manager to employee, and from employee to manager.

C

code of conduct - A set of rules defining acceptable and unacceptable behavior.

collaborative communication - Two-way, or interactive, communication, in which both parties participate.

D

decision-making leave - A short period of leave, usually paid, given to an employee who has committed a transgression, designed to encourage the employee to reflect on the problem and consider solutions.

disciplinary issue - A problem behavior that continues to occur even after the employee has been informed of the problem and the organization's expectations, and formal interventions have been conducted.

due process - A process for addressing issues that's reasonable and fair. Organizations can protect themselves legally by following due process when addressing employee performance problems.

E

emerging pattern - A pattern, or trend, that's becoming established. An emerging pattern of poor performance is evident if undesirable behavior is repeated on several occasions.

F

facts - Records of actual events, described without bias. Facts can be independently verified.

fast fix - A quick solution that doesn't require widespread change or significant effort.

final written warning - In a process of progressive discipline, the last written warning given to an employee. If required improvement doesn't occur in response to this warning, the employee will face a severe consequence such as termination of employment.

formal disciplinary action - Action taken in accordance with organizational protocols for disciplining employees and that's recorded in the employees' files. It's used in the case of serious breaches of company policies or in response to a persistent performance problem.

G

goal - A projected future outcome of a strategy.

I

informal intervention - Casual discussions about minor to moderate performance problems. The actions aren't recorded in employees' files.

initial written warning - In relation to handling employee performance problems, the second step in a process of progressive discipline. When a verbal warning fails to resolve poor performance, the next step is to issue an initial written warning to inform the employee that despite interventions, the performance problem still exists. It may prompt the employee to take the situation more seriously and represents evidence that an organization has followed due process.

J

job performance standard - A minimum level of work that an average but experienced employee is expected to perform.

K

key performance indicator - See KPI.

key result area - An area of work determined by management in which strong performance is considered critical.

KPI - Abbreviation for key performance indicator, a measurement of a key aspect of organizational performance.

M

management by walking around - The process of walking around the workplace, observing employees and engaging with them about their work.

mandated issues - Issues or behaviors that are clearly regulated by company policy and that require specified types of interventions.

minor to moderate performance issue - A performance problem that can be addressed informally; it isn't serious enough to warrant formal discipline and hasn't persisted over time despite management intervention.

monitoring - In the context of managing performance, the process of tracking employees' actual performance and comparing this to the expected performance to identify any discrepancies.

motivation - Drive or desire to achieve specific goals.

O

observation - The process of personally watching or listening to subjects' behavior to gather information. Managers may observe employees as part of the process of monitoring their performance.

P

perceptions - Subjective views of events or situations. They're shaped by people's world views and backgrounds.

performance appraisal - Evaluation of an employee's actual performance in relation to agreed expectations.

performance criterion - A requisite skill or behavior.

performance management - The ongoing, collaborative process of planning and monitoring performance, and of giving employees feedback to help them optimize their performance.

performance problem - An issue that prevents an employee from meeting work-related expectations.

performance transgression - A failure to comply with performance-related requirements or expectations.

persistent performance problem - A performance problem that continues despite intervention, for example due to an employee's lack of skill or motivation.

probation - A specified period in which an employee is expected to demonstrate improved performance. If no improvement occurs within this period, the employee will face a consequence such as dismissal.

problem frequency - How often a problem is occurring.

problem impact - The consequences, or effects, of a problem.

problem scope - The extent of a problem, including what's occurring and where, and who's involved in or affected by the problem.

progressive discipline - A process in which increasingly severe penalties are imposed for repeated performance transgressions. Stages in a progressive discipline process typically include issuing a verbal warning, issuing an initial written warning, and then issuing a final written warning. The final warning may be followed by termination of employment.

R

representative sampling - The use of subsets of data that accurately represent relevant characteristics of the full data set.

S

self-assessment - Evaluation of one's own performance.

self-reporting - Reporting on one's own performance.

suspension without pay - A period of unpaid leave given as punishment for a disciplinary offence.

V

verbal warning - In relation to handling employee performance problems, the first step in a process of progressive discipline. It involves a manager informing an employee of the need to improve to avoid further disciplinary action. Typically a verbal warning is followed by a written warning if no improvement occurs.

W

work expectation - The average or desired amount of work an average but experienced employee is expected to perform.

written warning - In relation to handling employee performance problems, a formal, written warning that an employee's performance must improve if the employee is to avoid further disciplinary action. Typically an initial written warning is followed by a final written warning if no improvement occurs.

#

360-degree feedback - Feedback about an employee's performance that is collected from a range of people the employee interacts with. For example, this may include the employee's manager, colleagues, and subordinates, as well as customers and suppliers.

www.ingramcontent.com/pod-product-compliance
Lightning Source LLC
Chambersburg PA
CBHW020904180526
45163CB00007B/2618